TRIBAL CO-OPERATIVES IN INDIA

TRIBAL CO-OPERATIVES IN INDIA

Dr. H.R. Krishnaiah Gowda
M.A., Ph.D

SERIALS PUBLICATIONS
New Delhi

Deputy Registrar of Co-operative Societies
Mandya, Karnataka India

First Published 2007

ISBN: 81-86771-18-2

Published by

Head Office : **SERIALS PUBLICATIONS**
4, B.S.S. Hall, Khyber Pass Market,
Civil Lines, Delhi–110054 (India)
Fax: 91-11-23812678
e-mail: serials@satyam.net.in

Branch Office : 4830/24, Prahlad Street, Ansari Road,
Darya Ganj, New Delhi-110002 (India)
Phone: 23245225

Printed at : Tarun Offset Printers, (Delhi)

FOREWORD

I am extremely happy to write a few words as Foreword to the book "Tribal Co-operatives in India" authored by Dr. H.R. Krishnaiah Gowda.

The Present work is indeed an important addition to the literature on tribal Co-operatives in India. The Various Programmes launched by both National and State Governments to bring tribals to main stream economic life are well known. Research indicates that these Programmes have hardly reached targeted group. In fact many of these programmes have been resisted by the tribals.

Dr. Krishnaiah Gowda has chosen to probe deep into one such programme, namely Co-operatives. Special types of co-operatives have been organised throughout the length and breadth of the country to ameliorate the economic conditions of the poor tribals. Large sized Adivasi Multipurpose Co-operative Societies (LAMPS) are one of the types of organisations in this direction.

Lamps are organised in some states as a result of Bawa Committee recommendations. These Co-operatives are expected to serve the needs of tribals exclusively. The author tries to take a close look at the working of these societies in general with a particular focus on their working in the state of Karnataka. The present work is a pains taking one. The work is of research type. Being a person working in the Co-operative department Dr. Krishnaiah Gowda could have access to the original documents and data relating to LAMPS. He has also undertaken an extensive tour to visit Tribal Co-operatives in different states. This has given him an insight into the practical problems of LAMPS. I should write that Dr. Krishnaiah Gowda has been impassionate and candid in his analysis. He does not hesitate to point out that "organisational base of LAMPS is weak. Majority of the directors of the board are incapable of taking decisions and understanding the issues at large. The most horrible and an unimaginable factor is that majority of the ex-officio directors do not attend board meetings. It is a pity that persons who have been directors by virtue of their office and who are carefully chosen to represent the government on the board have taken the things for granted and have shown utter contempt about the activities and administration of tribal societies."

Dr. Krishnaiah Gowda's recommendaitons to improve the working of tribal Societies are also worth noting. It is my earnest wish that the policy makers take serious note of these recommendations. One will have no choice but to accept the observation of the author of this book that half hearted measures to improve the Tribal Co-operatives will not benefit any one and the tribal Co-operatives will have no special place and cannot carve a place of their own in the integral Co-operative movement of the country.

The author's indepth study of LAMPS in Karnataka needs special mention. He has probed deep into the structural and organisational aspects of LAMPS in Karnataka. One has to agree with the author that there is wide scope for making LAMPS in Karnataka State robust and viable.

These organisations are capable of strengthening the economic basis of poor tribals. But it requires strong political and bureaucratic commitment. Many of the structural weaknesses can be overcome if the author's recommendations are implemented.

The present work is a very useful addition tot he literature on tribals in general and Co-operative movement in particular. The author's organisation of the book is appreciable and the style of writing in lucid. I earnestly hope that persons interested in Co-operative movement and in tribals welcome this productive and useful work. I expect many more works from Dr. Krishnaiah Gowda on Co-operative movement, as he has the advantage of having a Kaleidoscopic look, being a person belonging to the Department of Co-operation.

C.K. Renukarya
Prof. of Economics (Retd)
University of Mysore

PREFACE

This study is a revised version of my doctoral thesis approved by the University of Mysore. It is my pleasant duty to record my deep sense of gratitude to all those who have helped me in completing this work.

I am extremely grateful to Dr. C.K. Renukarya, Professor of Economics, my beloved teacher, a scholar and an econometrician, for his expert advice and invaluable guidance. He has been kind enough to contribute the foreword.

I am grateful to the Department of Co-operation, Government of Karnataka and to the University of Mysore for having accorded me permission to carry out this study and to publish it in the form of a book.

My warmest regards are due to Sri. H. Vishwanath, Hon'ble Minister for Co-operation, Government of Karnataka for his constant encouragement. I acknowledge with humility the encouraging words of Sri. A. Ramaswamy, I.A.S. Principal Secretary, Department of Co-operation, Government of Karnataka, Bangalore, in instilling confidence to carryout academic work.

I owe a debt of gratitude to Sri. Siddaiah, I.A.S., Registrar of Co-operative Societies, Karnataka State,

Bangalore, Smt. Shehar Banu, Gazetted Assistant to the Registrar of Co-operative Societies, and to Sri. G. Jayram, Private Secretary to Hon'ble Minister for Co-operation, Government of Karnataka, for their unflinching support.

I express my sincere gratitude to Shri. G.R. Krishna Das, Joint Registrar of Co-operative Societies, Command Area Development Authority, Mysore, Sri. K. T. Jayaramu, Joint Registrar of Co-operative Societies, Mysore Region, Mysore, Shri. B.A. Mahadevappa, Managing Director, District Central Co-operative Bank, Madikeri, Sri. H. Jayadev, Secretary, Karnataka State Co-operative Agricultural and Rural Development Bank, Bangalore, Sri. B.K. Yadunath and Sri. K.R. Dharmappa, Joint Registrar of Co-operative Societies, for their invaluable suggestions.

Grateful acknowledgement is due to Sri. K.A. Jadhav, Zonal Manager, Zonal Office, TRIFED, Mumbai, but for whose timely help and suggestions, it would not have been possible for me to complete this study.

I am heavily indebted to the Chief Executives and officials of all the 21 Large-sized Adivasi Multi-purpose Co-operative societies in Karnataka for providing me valuable and relevant information and materials on the working of these societies. But for their timely assistance and masterly interpretation of facts, this work would have remained an unaccomplished endeavour. I am also thankful to the management, both elected and official, of these societies for having provided me useful insights into the working of these societies. I extend my thanks also to the management and officials of the LAMPS of other states particularly of Elagiri Hills, Tamil Nadu and Karanjali, Maharashtra, for providing me useful information during my visits.

I acknowledge with thanks the help. I received from Smt. K. Rajamma, President, Sri. K.M. Chandraiah,

Managing Director and Sri. Krishnegowda, Manager, Karnataka State LAMPS Federation, Mysore.

Expert comments offered by the evaluators of my thesis—Dr. Oumar Bouare of Human Sciences Research Council, Pretoria, South Africa, and Dr. Francis Cherunilam, professor, school of Management Studies, Cochin University of Science and Technology, Kochin, Kerala, stood me in good stead while improvising the study and bringing it out in the form of this book.

I profusely thank Dr. M.G. Basavaraja, Assistant Professor of Economics, University of Mysore and a host of my friends and well wishers whose assistance and encouragement were a source of inspiration to me throughout this work. Affection showered on me by my wife Mrs. S.M. Kusuma and my beloved children Manjeswara and Bhagyalakshmi strengthened my commitment to carryout this study.

I find immense pleasure in dedicating this book to my parents who played a decisive role in my becoming a serious student of knowledge.

My sincere thanks are due to Sri. S.K. Jha, Director, Serials Publications, Delhi, who unhesistatinsly came forward to publish this book. He and the members of his publication have been kind enough to bring out this book earnestly and in a record short time.

Mandya **H.R. Krishnaiah Gowda**

CONTENTS

To

My Parents

CHAPTER — 1

INTRODUCTION AND DESIGN OF THE STUDY

Introduction

Co-operation as an economic system is considered to be a golden mean between capitalism and socialism. It developed in many countries of the world out of the felt needs of the people. Co-operative movement in India took its birth in the early years of the twentieth century, and with the passing of the 'Co-operative Societies Act' in 1904, a statutory framework was provided to it. There are innumerable types of co-operatives in India such as of credit, consumers, processing, marketing, housing, etc., as also to serve different sections of people. In other words, co-operative institutions in India as elsewhere have been organised to take care of different activities as also for various sections of people. Large—sized Adivasi Multi-Purpose Co-operative Societies, shortly called LAMPS, are one of the many types of co-operative institutions in India which are being organised of late. These are the Societies, by name and in deed, for the Adivasis or tribal people. Hence, tribal co-operatives in India are also called large-sized Adivasi Multi-purpose co-operative societies.

LAMPS are co-operative institutions which have been organised to serve as a focal point for welfare of the tribal community. Creation of LAMPS covering almost all possible avenues of economic services to the tribal community was the main import of the Bawa Committee on Co-operative Structure in Tribal Development Agency Project.[1] The Committee was set up by the Ministry of Agriculture, Government of India, in 1971, to study the problem of exploitation of tribals and to suggest an institutional framework to provide credit and other economic needs of tribals. The committee headed by Shri K.S. Bawa, Joint Secretary in the Ministry of Co-operation, Government of India, in its report which was submitted in 1973, recommended that LAMPS should be established covering one block/tehsil with a requisite number of branches to provide a package of services to the tribal people at a single point.[2]

The committee was of the view that "a tribal should not be required to approach too many institutions for assistance. The primary society which deals with individual tribals should, therefore, provide all the important services required by him, namely, provision of short term and medium term production credit, and consumption credit to be recovered from sale of minor forest produce, distribution of inputs and consumer goods, marketing of minor forest and agricultural produce. These services should be organised at 'Hat' (Market) level as the tribal comes to the 'hat' periodically".[3] It was on the lines of these suggestions and of the growing needs of prevailing local conditions that a new pattern of primary co-operatives was introduced in tribal areas, and they are called LAMPS.

A LAMPS is a bigger society especially designed for tribal regions. These bigger units were either formed afresh or by assimilating all the scattered varieties of primary credit, consumer and other co-operative societies working in the area of a block, or in many cases even a bigger market place (hat) under a tribal development project. The main objectives with which the LAMPS have been organised are liberating the tribals from the clutches of money lenders through supply of production and consumption credit, to provide an assured market to tribal produce, to promote subsidy-cum-loan production scheme to develop the tribal economy, and to supply essential commodities and agricultural inputs to tribal people.

The Bawa Committee very explicitly suggested that "suitable higher level organisations should be pressed into service to support, supervise and guide the activities of societies at the primary level".[4] In accordance with the recommendations of the Committee, States such as Andhra Pradesh, Bihar, Madhya Pradesh, Maharashtra, Manipur, Rajasthan, Orissa and West Bengal have established Tribal Development Corporations/Federations to support the activities of LAMPS.

As per the Bawa Committee recommendations, LAMPS are being organised since the year 1974. But in many states, co-operative societies to cater to the needs exclusively of tribal people were being formed even since the 1960s. These institutions were then usually called 'Forest Labour Co-operative Societies' since these were formed to cater to the needs of labourers engaged in collection and sale of forest produce. With the suggestions of the study team headed by K.S. Bawa, the existing societies were renamed and new societies were organised as Large-sized Adivasi Multi-Purpose Co-operative Societies. Though these societies have grown both in their number and in terms of volume of business, information on their working is not easily available. Performance of LAMPS in many states is really dismal. The services they render as well as their profit earning capacity in many pockets is also poor. But in many areas LAMPS have been rendering a remarkable service and have been able to diversify their activities. Since these are the co-operative institutions formed to attend to the needs of exclusively tribal people, it is of great significance to investigate their working, the reasons for their failure and the factors behind their success.

Importance of LAMPS

Tribals are a section of people who are weak socially and economically. They have no easy access to necessaries of life and other requirements from nearby places and at reasonable prices. They are actually at a loss to find a market to dispose of the produce they grow or collect.

In these circumstances the government came forward to take up many measures and to implement a large number of schemes to bring about social and economic betterment of the tribal community. Organisation of LAMPS to serve the needs of the tribal people is one such important measure. The LAMPS have been organised as part of the tribal sub-plan which was devised in the year 1974-75 to give a preferential treatment to the tribal society.

LAMPS have been providing marketing services. They purchase minor forest and agricultural produce from the members for a certain price and sell them in different channels. They also advance short-term and medium-term loans to members at comparatively low rate of interest for productive purposes. In many states these societies have undertaken the function of public distribution of essential commodities. It is of interest to note that many LAMPS have opened retail shops to sell daily requirements, and cloth. A large number of LAMPS also sell agricultural inputs of all types viz., fertilisers, seeds, implements, pesticides and fodder.

Through their functioning, the LAMPS have been able to create a large number of employment opportunities, to generate income and to provide a fair price for agricultural and minor forest produce. They have been helpful in making value addition to the products through processing and storage activities.

LAMPS have gone a long way in opening up new horizons in the life of tribal people as explained in the foregoing paras. But the other side of the picture is that LAMPS have been facing innumerable problems. Performance of many a LAMPS is indeed dismal. These societies have been facing many problems and are at the mercy of the government, middlemen and apex level institutions.

Organisation of the Book

The book is organised into six chapters as outlined below.

Chapter one deals with introduction and design of the study. It covers importance of tribal Co-operatives.

A bird's eye view of the working of LAMPS in different states and union territories of India in which they are existing, is undertaken in the second chapter. The genesis and relevance of LAMPS and different aspects of their growth in some selected years are dealt with.

Growth of LAMPS in Karnataka in their different aspects is analysed in chapter three. It involves a quantitative and qualitative assessment. Failures on the part of the LAMPS in Karnataka and the reasons there of are discussed in detail.

The fourth Chapter makes an indepth study of the working of eight selected LAMPS in Karnataka. It is a case study of the selected LAMPS. For a proper sampling, many criteria such as intensity of dependence on forests, accumulated profit or loss, special activities undertaken etc., were taken into account while choosing the societies for case studies. For example, four societies which are heavily forest-dependent, and four societies which are not heavily forest-dependent are taken. Broad conclusions about the working, success and failures of these societies, are arrived at in the course of case studies.

A suitable and an operative model for successful and proper working of LAMPS is advocated in the fifth chapter. Collection and sale of minor forest produce (MFP) is the major income generating activity of LAMPS. There are a few views that the LAMPS should concentrate only on MFP business. However, for a successful working of the society as a commercial venture and to serve the members effectively, diversification of activities is seen as essential. It is in this background, it has been found essential to advocate a workable model for LAMPS.

The sixth chapter gives a resume of the study and draws conclusions on the basis of earlier findings. Further, relevant suggestions for improving the working of LAMPS in India in general, and in Karnataka State in particular, are offered in this chapter.

REFERENCES

1. Guru, H.N.-*"Tribal Co-operatives in Madhaya Pradesh: The Lamps"*, The Co-operator, April 15, 1984.
2. Government of India, *Summary Report of the Study team on Co-operative Structure in Tribal Development Agency Projects,* 1973, p.5.
3. Ibid., pp. 2-3.
4. Ibid., p.3.

CHAPTER — 2

Working of Tribal Co-operatives in India-An Overview

In this chapter an attempt is made to analyse the genesis of Large-sized Adivasi Multi-purpose Co-operative Societies, or tribal Co-operatives in India, as well as rationale behind their organisation. Attempt is made also to take a view of the tribal problems and needs, to have a bird's eye view of growth of these institutions in India, to briefly review the working of these societies in different states of the Indian Union and to suggest a proper link-up between these societies and the concerned federal organisations.

Large-sized Adivasi Multi-Purpose Co-operative Societies, shortly called LAMPS, were visualised as vehicles of tribal development. The tribal economy is characterised by backwardness, acute lack of infrastructural facilities, isolation and cultural stagnation. To cap it all, the people living in tribal areas are by and large illiterate and undernourished. The lives of the tribes is lost in hills and forests. Tribal people have made them their common abode. This voluminously explains the reasons for the problems of the tribal economy.

Economic, social and cultural backwardness is the hallmark of the tribal system. Since tribals are isolated from the rest of the world their social and economic backwardness can be easily explained. Their economic backwardness is partly owing to their alienation and partly because of various other reasons. Lack of opportunities on the part of the tribals to harness the available resources to their advantage, want of right over the resources and their extraction, absence of transportation and communication facilities, scarcity of employment avenues and lack of awareness among the people, are some of the important reasons for economic backwardness of the tribal system. It is imperative to note that economic upliftment will certainly go a long way in ameliorating different other problems haunting the tribal system. Hence many important measures which can help provide economic strength to the tribals were pertinently thought of by the Government and the planners. Such measures include providing rights over and accessibility to extract and market forest products, opening avenues for Job opportunities, providing credit, housing, irrigational and other facilities to the tribal community. It is in this background, formation of Large-sized Adivasi Multi-Purpose Co-operative Societies has been considered to be a path-breaking measure.

The Genesis of LAMPS

Co-operation as an economic system has been considered to be the best instrument to ameliorate socio-economic conditions of the weaker sections of the community. Co-operative form of organisations have been the most suitable agencies to bring about a radical change in the conditions of the tribal community. The tribals were being exploited by money-lenders, middlemen and traders for a very long period. Owing to insufficient arrangement for credit and for marketing of agricultural and forest produce in the tribal areas, it was natural that tribals would fall into the clutches of this exploiting lot. It was therefore necessary that the tribals were saved from middlemen, usurious money-lenders and avaricious traders. Tribals had to be ensured a fair price for their agricultural and forest produce.

Various commissions and committees appointed by the Government of India and different state governments to suggest measures for tribal development have more specifically recommended that co-operatives could be suitable agencies to bring about transformation in the tribal economy.

The social welfare team of the committee on plan projects (1959) recommended that commercial exploitation of forest be entrusted to co-operatives rather than to contractors.

The Scheduled Area and Scheduled Tribes Commission also known as Dhebar Commission[1] (1960-61) had recommended that the sale and marketing of the produce and supply of tribal people's needs at reasonable price should receive special attention through co-operatives.

The Special Working Group on Co-operation of Backward classes[2] (1962) attributed slow development of co-operative development in tribal areas to structural weaknesses, operational defects, management problems, faulty procedures and adoption of business methods and practices not suitable to tribals.

A Study Team appointed by the Government of India[3] (1971) with Shri. K.S. Bawa, Joint Secretary in the Union Department of Co-operation as the Chairman, recommended organisation of Large-sized Adivasi Multi-purpose Co-operative Societies in tribal areas to provide their tribal members, production as well as consumption credit, to undertake marketing of agricultural and minor forest produces and to distribute consumer goods as well as agricultural inputs so that the tribal could secure all facilities under one roof. The Bawa Team also known as the "Study Team on Co-operative Structure in Tribal Development Project Areas" had the specific responsibility of suggesting ways and means to the development of tribal economy. The Government of India had sanctioned six projects for tribal development in the states of Andhra Pradesh, Bihar, Orissa and Madhya Pradesh. The districts selected were Srikakulam in Andhra Pradesh, Singhbhum in Bihar, Ganjam and Koraput in Orissa and Bastar-I (Bantewada) and Bastar-II (Konta) in Madhya Pradesh. The outlay on core programme of economic development was Rs. 1.50 crore for each project, and another Rs. 50 Lakhs for each project for arterial roads.[4] As provision of credit for various production programmes and arrangements for marketing of agricultural and forest produce on co-operative basis for the benefit of tribals are of crucial importance to their economic development, the Government appointed this study team with specific terms of reference. The committee submitted its report in 1973.

The recommendations of the Bawa Committee regarding organisation of LAMPS were far reaching and vociferous. It was on the basis of these suggestions and of the growing needs of prevailing local conditions, that a new pattern of primary co-operative institutions was introduced in tribal areas. The large-sized Adivasi Multipurpose Co-operative Societies were in the beginning also called 'Large-sized Adimjati Multi-purpose Societies in some states like Madhya Pradesh,[5] the words Adimjati and Adivasi being synonymous.

The Rationale Behind Organisation of LAMPS

Need for integrated services was emphasised by the All-India Rural Credit Survey Committee (1951-52). Its indispensability in the context of small and marginal farmers, and especially weaker sections, was prominently stressed in the interim report (1973) of the National Commission on Agriculture. The Bawa Committee inspired by earlier deliberations and also by their keen observation of the prevalent situation in tribal areas, very explicitly suggested that "a tribal should not be required to approach too many institutions for assistance. The primary society which deals with individual tribals should, therefore, provide all the important services required by him, namely, provisions of short and medium-term production credit, and consumption credit to be recovered from sale of minor forest produce, distribution of inputs and consumer goods, and marketing of minor forest and agricultural produce ..[6] The committee in its basic approach and recommendations goes further and states that "minor forest produce is a major source of income to the tribals, and this also constitutes a major area of exploitation of tribals by middlemen. It is, therefore, important that co-operatives of Adivasis should have the exclusive right of collection of minor forest produce and the Adivasis should be assured, through their cooperatives, a reasonable price for the minor forest produce collected by them"[7]

The collection and sale of minor forest products such as honey, tender leaves, amla fruit, soapnut, lichen, tree gums etc., had been a subsidiary occupation of tribal communities right from the Pre-British period. As shifting cultivation and hunting were banned and the tribals got pushed into a monetised exchange economy, their dependence on minor forest products for income increased, even as their access to forests declined. But they were at the mercy of middlemen and MFP contractors, who controlled access to markets, or forests, or both.[8]

The Bawa Committee recommended that LAMPS should be organised in tribal areas on the lines of Farmers' Service Societies (FSS) providing a package of services such as credit for production and consumption needs, technical guidance for agriculture and arranging for marketing of their produce.

Historically, tribal communities were characterised by a lifestyle distinct from agrarian communities. They subsisted on some combination of shifting cultivation, hunting and gathering of forest products: all activities closely linked with forests. Their cultures celebrated and fostered this close bond with nature, while also emphasising communal ownership and consumption, closely knit Kinship structures, and minimal hierarchies.[9]

Co-operation as a form of economic organisation is ideally suited to the tribal life and the economy. Since the tribals are economically backward and exploited, socially handicapped and have a greater sense of homogenity, the cooperative form of organisation may by and large be the most suitable agency for bringing about a thorough transformation in their economic and social conditions.

LAMPS as instruments of tribal development were being organised in India since 1974. Even before Bawa committee recommendations, some cooperative societies on these lines were formed in some states particularly since the First Five Year Plan. They were called 'Forest Labour Contract Societies' and also 'Labour Contact Multipurpose Societies.' They had as their main objective collection and sale of minor forest produces and catering to the credit and marketing needs of the tribal people.

But the recommendations of the Bawa Committee gave new impetus to the organisation of LAMPS as they enumerated the broad objectives with which the LAMPS have to be established and the direction in which they have to grow. By 1989, 2912 LAMPS had been established across the country. Out of this more than 80 percent of the societies were in the five states of Madhya Pradesh, Bihar, Maharashtra, Rajasthan and Orissa that have large tribal population.

The broad objectives with which the LAMPS have been organised are as follows:

1. Promotion of subsidy-cum-loan production scheme in the fields of agriculture, horticulture, animal husbandry, irrigation, forestry, cottage and village industries.
2. Liberating the tribals from the clutches of money lenders through supply of production and consumption credit.
3. Purchase from tribals their surplus agricultural produce and forest produce.
4. Supply of essential commodities and agricultural inputs to tribal people.

The LAMPS is a bigger society especially designed for tribal regions. These bigger units were formed by assimilating all the scattered varieties of primary credit, consumer and other co-operative societies working in the area of block or in many cases even a bigger market place under a tribal development project. In a large number of areas new LAMPS were organised at the block level.

The Bawa Committee had proposed setting up of state level tribal development co-operative corporations/ Federations. The primary level societies were to be affiliated to the apex corporations for getting organisational and financial support for their marketing, supply and distributional functions. In accordance with these recommendations, States such as Andhra Pradesh,

Bihar, Madhya Pradesh, Maharashtra, Manipur, Rajasthan, Orissa and West Bengal have established Tribal Development Corporations/Federations.

Co-operative institutions to cater to the needs exclusively of tribal areas have much relevance. The history of man as a social being begins in small tribal groups. It is generally said that if co-operation has to succeed it has to first succeed among tribals. Because the very way of tribals' life is based on leadership and participation. Since tribals are at a loss to avail credit facilities and to procure necessaries of life and to have a suitable avenue to sell their products, creation of Large-sized Adivasi Multi-purpose co-operative Societies to cater to the needs of those people under one roof has acquired greater relevance.

The Tribal Sub-plan-TSP

The concept of tribal sub-plan needs special mention in this context. Large-sized Adivasi Multi-purpose Co-operative Societies have been introduced as part of this plan. The tribal sub-plan is a comprehensive frame work aiming at socio-economic development of scheduled tribes and their protection from exploitation by other groups of the society. As the concept itself indicates, it is a sub-plan under a comprehensive national plan targeted towards welfare of the socially and economically neglected class, i.e., tribals. With the inclusion of tribal development as the seventh point of the 20 point programme, adopted by the Government of India in 1975, tribal sub-plan strategy received an added momentum.

There are various factors which contribute to backwardness and economic deprivation of the tribals. But the most important factor has been exploitation of the tribals by money lenders-cum-traders. One of the main objectives of the tribal sub-plan is to protect the tribals from this blatant and rampant exploitation. A number of measures have been introduced under the Tribal sub-plan which can help the tribals to attain economic and social welfare.

The tribal sub-plan strategy emphasises that the distinctive ethos and identity of a tribal group need to be kept in the fore while planning for socio-economic development. Basically, the tribal sub-plan aims at creating at the project level a pool of financial resources for making, through well-knit co-ordinated administrative structure, attempts at execution of well conceived policies and programmes rooted in the cultural traditions and natural resource endowment of the tribal area and the people.

'Scheduled Area' and 'Integrated Tribal Development Project' (ITDP) are the two important concepts in the purview of the tribal sub-plan.

It has been the policy of the Government of India to declare tribal area as Scheduled Areas where more than 50 percent of the population of that area belongs to scheduled tribes. And such area is taken up for preferential treatment by means of various schemes and measures to bring about development of the area and the people. This norm was subsequently relaxed in many states and according to the new norm any area having a scheduled tribes population of ten thousand and more was taken up for special treatment and an integrated Tribal Development Project was formed in that area. Many government departments are involved under this project and funds are pumped through these departments for tribal welfare. Co-operation is one such department and resources are given to LAMPS for training programme and other measures undertaken for tribal welfare.

A Glimpse Of the Tribal Problems and Needs

Scheduled Tribes (STs) mean such tribes or tribal communities as are deemed so under Article 342 of the Constitution of India. A tribe is a social group in which there are many clans, nomadic bands, sub-groups having a definite geographical area, a separate language, a distinct culture and a common political organisation or a feeling of common determination against strangers. A tribal group is a traditional social group of a simple kind, the members of which speak a common language or a dialect and act together for certain common socio-economic purposes. The tribal group exhibits a relatively uniform culture or way of life and a tradition of common descent. They generally live away from civilised world in the inaccessible regions lying in the forests and hills. They pursue primitive occupations such as gleaning, hunting and gathering of forest produce. Many of them are bonded slaves under landlords, money lenders and contractors. They also work in plantations, mines and other enterprises to eke out their livelihood.

There are about 200 million tribals in the world forming roughly about 4 percent of the global population.

India has the largest concentration of tribal people anywhere in the world, except perhaps Africa. According to the 1991 census, they account for about 68 million and the percentage of scheduled tribe population to the total population has been 8.08. About 19 percent of the total area in India is the tribal region. This is mostly concentrated in hilly and forest parts as well as in the plain areas of Madhya Pradesh, Bihar, Maharashtra, Orissa, Rajasthan, Uttar Pradesh, West Bengal, Andhra Pradesh, Tamil Nadu, Karnataka, Jammu and Kashmir and many union territories.

The following table indicates the percentage of scheduled tribe population to the total population of India.

Table 2.1

Scheduled Tribe Population as Percentage of Total Population, 1991[10]

	State or Union Territory	*Percentage of ST Population to the total*
	India	8.08
	States	
1.	Andhra Pradesh	6.31
2.	Arunachal Pradesh	63.66
3.	Assam	12.82
4.	Bihar	7.66
5.	Goa	0.03
6.	Gujarat	14.92
7.	Haryana	–
8.	Himachal Pradesh	4.22
9.	Karnataka	4.26
10.	Kerala	1.10
11.	Madhya Pradesh	23.27
12.	Maharashtra	9.27
13.	Manipur	34.41
14.	Meghalaya	85.53
15.	Mizoram	94.75
16.	Nagaland	87.70
17.	Orissa	22.21
18.	Punjab	–
19.	Rajasthan	12.44
20.	Sikkim	22.36
21.	Tamil Nadu	1.03
22.	Tripura	30.95
23.	Uttar Pradesh	0.21
24.	West Bengal	5.59

(Table Contd.)

	State or Union Territory	Percentage of ST Population to the total
Union Territories		
1.	Andaman and Nicobar Islands	9.54
2.	Chandigarh	–
3.	Dadra and Nagar Havelli	78.99
4.	Daman and Diu	11.54
5.	Delhi	–
6.	Lakshadweep	93.15
7.	Pondicherry	–

* Excludes figures of Jammu and Kashmir where 1991 census was not taken.

The scheduled castes and scheduled tribes together constitute 24.56 percent of the total population of the country excluding Jammu and Kashmir. The separate percentage figures for scheduled castes and scheduled tribes work out to be 16.48 percent and 8.08 percent respectively. Some of the states and Union Territories where population is predominantly scheduled tribes arranged in descending order of percentage distribution are Mizoram (94.75 percent), Lakshadweep (93.15 percent), Nagaland (87.70 percent), Meghalaya (85.53 percent), Dadra and Nagar Haveli (78.99 percent) and Arunachal Pradesh (63.66 percent).

Among tribes there are a large number of communities. In India the total number of tribal communities is reported to be 642 and several of them have become extinct or merged with other communities as the tendency for fusion and fission among tribal population is found to be a continuous process. Out of 642 communities only 428 communities speaking as many as 106 languages have so far been notified as scheduled in 22 states and 4 union territories. A vast majority of the 106 languages the tribals speak do not have script.

Some of the important communities of scheduled tribes found in different states and union territories of India are Gond, Iatapus, Koya, Valmiki, Chakma, Garo, Asur, Kora, Dhodia, Varli, Koracha, Koraga, Hasalaru, Soliga, Marathi Naik, Gowdlu, Yerava, Baiga, Kathodi, Irular, Adiyan, Malasar, Paniyan, Hira, Kuki, Naga, Banjara, Bedia, etc.,[11]

The Dhebar Commission divided the tribals into the following four categories:[12]

(i) Those that are living in the remotest corners and for that reason are almost in a primitive stage;

(ii) Those in the shifting cultivation stage;

(iii) Those who have taken to regular agriculture; and

(iv) Those that have been assimilated.

The first two categories of tribals happen to be still primitive, the last two categories are relatively forward and have a certain base for living. But it does not do justice to say that the last two categories do not face any problems. The first two categories lead a primitive and nomadic life, the other two categories, though are assimilated and have taken to regular agriculture, are in the throes of many a problem.

Cultural stagnation of the tribal society is one of the main problems the tribals are facing. They are isolated from the vast changes that the forces of modernisation have brought in their wake.

Tribals have been at the jaws of starvation for centuries together. Malnutrition, unhygienic living conditions and epidemic diseases over the years have reduced many of them to a condition of hopelessness.

Tribal economy is largely dependent upon forest and agriculture. In the last three decades forests have been denuded forcing the tribals to reduce their dependence on forests. The tribal agriculture is largely associated with traditional methods of cultivation and the cropping pattern is more diversified. Lack of irrigation facilities and other agricultural inputs has compounded their woes. As a result, the family income of tribals is miserably low.

Another major problem of the tribals is chronic indebtedness. It is estimated that about 86 per cent of tribal population is in deep debt. Tribal people by and large depend upon only money-lenders for their financial needs. An analysis of their indebtedness reveals a vulnerable economy enmeshed in a vicious circle of poverty, low productivity and chronic indebtedness compounded by blatant exploitation by traders and money lenders.

The problem of illiteracy is striking on the face of the tribal populace. The percentage of literacy among them as per 1991 census is as low as 29.60. This percentage varies from state to state. The highest percentage of literacy among tribals is recorded in Mizoram with 82.71 percent, followed by Nagaland with 60.59 percent. Andhra Pradesh has the lowest percentage with 17.16.

The Dhebar Commission agreed that one of the major problems in the tribal areas is that of shifting cultivation, and it is not an ideal method. Under this system, the forest and undergrowth are cleared and the slash is burned. Soil is not turned up with plough, and seeds are either broadcast or sown into dibbled holes. Usually two or three crops in as many years are raised on such plots and thereafter the cultivation shifts to another new plot which is similarly treated. The yield depends on the presence of humus on the original forest floor and the minerals obtained on burning of the slash. So the same area is cultivated as long as it yields subsistence. Since the forest area is limited, sooner or later shifting cultivation returns to the same area. Yield in the second rotation is less, because the fertility does not build up to the original level and the soil is subject to soil erosion processes. So in every cycle rotation gets shorter as cultivation is done for a fewer number of years in the same area. Increase in numbers is also responsible for shortening cycles. The cycle of shifting cultivation thus gets shorter and shorter, and erosion takes heavier and heavier toll resulting in deteriorating economic condition of the shifting cultivators.[13]

It is generally viewed that shifting cultivation has come down to a large extent and it exists only in some pockets of tribal regions. According to a study shifting cultivation was estimated to cover 26.7 million acres of land and was practised by 3.55 lakh families in early 1980s.[14]

Settled agriculture is the predominant source of livelihood among overwhelming majority of the tribals. But even in areas where they live with non-tribals, the lands cultivated by them are comparatively infertile and less productive.

Added to the problem of indebtedness, another form of exploitation is land alienation, i.e., transfer of lands from tribals to non-tribals. In recent years, many of the fertile lands in the tribal belt gradually got transferred to the self-styled land lords, whose average holdings ranged from 5 to 90 acres, while the average land holding of the tribals was as low as 0.66 acres.[15]

Coupled with all these problems the tribal people do not have easy access to necessaries of life and other requirements from nearby places and at reasonable prices. It is difficult for them to find a market to dispose of the surplus produce they grow or collect.

The Dhebar Commission felt that the new democratic state was discharging the responsibility of development and welfare of the tribal people and as a consequence the tribal problem had become an integral part of the Indian people. The Shily A. Team (1969) highlighted the tribal problem as a product of poverty, malnutrition, neglect, ill-treatment, exploitation etc., and called for measures for development which suited the ethnic characteristics, cultural practices and technological levels of the scheduled tribes.[16]

Organisation of Large-sized Adivasi Multi-purpose Co-operative Societies was visualised as a prominent measure to redress the grievances of the tribal people and to bring about economic transformation in the tribal society.

Progress of LAMPS in India

The Large-sized Adivasi Multi-purpose Co-operative Societies are being organised in different states and Union Territories of India as an important step in improving the economic and social conditions of the tribal people.

The following table indicates the number of LAMPS in different states and union territories and membership in them.

Table 2.2 shows that LAMPS are in existence in sixteen states i.e., Arunachal Pradesh, Assam, Bihar, Gujarat, Karnataka, Kerala, Madhya Pradesh, Maharashtra, Manipur, Mizoram, Nagaland, Orissa, Rajasthan, Tamil Nadu, Tripura and Uttar Pradesh and in two Union Territories of Dadra and Nagar Haveli and Daman and Diu.

The total number of LAMPS in existence in India as in 1998 has been 4423. Madhya Pradesh has the highest number of these institutions with 1073 and the union territory of Daman and Diu has the lowest with Just One.

The LAMPS had a total membership of 59.56 lakhs as at the end of March 1998. The corresponding figure as at the end of March 1994 was 36.31 lakhs. This indicates that there was an increase in membership to the tune of 23.25 Lakhs in the years between1994 and 1998.

Table 2.2

Number of LAMPS in India and Membership in them (1998)

Sl. No.	*State / Union Territory*	*No. of LAMPS*	*Membership (in thousands)*
1.	Andaman and Nicobar Islands	–	–
2.	Andhra Pradesh	–	–
3.	Arunachal Pradesh	32	16
4.	Assam	39	30
5.	Bihar	474	716
6.	Dadra and Nagar Haveli	06	22
7.	Daman and Diu	01	04
8.	Goa	–	–
9.	Gujarat	270	308
10.	Haryana	–	–
11.	Himachal Pradesh	–	–
12.	Karnataka	21	60
13.	Kerala	759	461
14.	Madhya Pradesh	1073	1608
15.	Maharashtra	984	623
16.	Manipur	63	497
17.	Meghalaya	–	–
18.	Mizoram	12	NA
19.	Nagaland	29	NA
20.	Orissa	223	775
21.	Pondicherry	–	–
22.	Punjab	–	–
23.	Rajasthan	268	522
24.	Sikkim	–	–
25.	Tamil Nadu	11	71
26.	Tripura	56	133
27.	Uttar Pradesh	102	110
28.	West Bengal	–	–
	Total	**4423**	**5956**

Source: Statistical statements relating to the Co-operative Movement in India, NABARD, 1997-98, part-I Credit Societies, p. 210 and p. 219 and Tribal Co-operative System-A Study of North East India, 1992, p. 15.

An important aspect is that in some states and union territories LAMPS have enrolled scheduled caste people also as their members. The exceptions are the state of Karnataka and the union territory of Daman and Diu. In Karnataka all the 60,000 members of LAMPS as in 1997-98 belonged to scheduled tribes category, as also in Daman and Diu where all the 4,000 members belonged to this category. In other states and in the Union Territory of Dadra and Nagar Haveli, scheduled caste people also have found membership in the LAMPS.

Table 2.3 indicates status of members of LAMPS with regard to their agricultural holdings and occupation.

The figures in the table 2.4 indicate that loans and advances of LAMPS have decreased over the years. The sharpest decline can be seen from Rs. 238.76 crores in 1985 to Rs. 78.36 crores in 1994. One important reason for this trend is that over the years, LAMPS have slowed down their lending operations and have diversified their activities like sale of consumer articles and procurement and sale of minor forest produces. Declining trend in lending operations can be seen in many states particularly in Orissa where almost all LAMPS have gone into red, and in Maharashtra and Karnataka where more than 70 percent of the medium term loans advanced by LAMPS were not repaid by members, and hence many LAMPS discontinued the practice of advancing loans. However, there has been a slight increase in the quantum of loans and advances in the year 1995. Government patronage in the form of share capital has shown a steady increase over the years. It has risen from Rs. 18.60 crores in 1985 to Rs. 28.28 crores in 1989 and to Rs. 42.63 crores in 1994. But there has been a slight decrease of Rs. 5 Lakhs in 1995 which is not perceptible. Loans outstanding have come down from Rs. 188.83 crores in 1985 to Rs. 116.09

Table 2.3

Status of Members of LAMPS

(Number in Thousands)

Sl. No.	State/ Union Territory	Farmers with land holdings: Upto Two Hectares	Farmers with land holdings: Above Two Hectares	Agricultural Labourers	Rural Artisans	Others	Total
1.	Arunachal Pradesh	NA	NA	NA	NA	NA	NA
2.	Assam	NA	NA	NA	NA	NA	NA
3.	Bihar	405	158	55	86	7	711
4.	Dadra and Nagar Haveli	5	3	–	–	–	8
5.	Daman and Diu	1	–	1	–	1	3
6.	Gujarat	100	77	33	6	43	259
7.	Karnataka	17	1	12	4	22	56
8.	Madhya Pradesh	–	–	–	–	–	–
9.	Maharashtra	188	157	192	7	11	555
10.	Manipur	NA	NA	NA	NA	NA	NA
11.	Mizoram	NA	NA	NA	NA	NA	NA
12.	Nagaland	NA	NA	NA	NA	NA	NA
13.	Orissa	606	239	37	12	12	906
14.	Rajasthan	288	148	25	9	23	493
15.	Tamil Nadu	28	15	6	–	14	63
16.	Tripura	79	8	24	1	12	124

Source: Statistical statements relating to the Co-operative Movement in India, NABARD 1994-95, p. 331.

Table 2.4

Credit and Non-credit Business and Financial Position of LAMPS in Selected Years

(Rs. in Crores)

Sl. No.	*Particulars*	*1985*	*1989*	*1994*	*1995*
1.	Paid-up Capital (Total)	48.92	70.32	71.52	75.04
	(a) of which Government share capital	18.60	28.28	42.63	42.58
2.	Total Assets/Working Capital	–	–	288.18	322.05
3.	Reserves	17.20	–	28.79	31.26
4.	Deposits	8.40	12.06	21.78	27.38
5.	Borrowings	170.22	248.80	124.58	146.83
6.	Loans and Advances (Total)	238.76	121.17	78.36	89.83
	(a) Short-Term Loans	200.15	90.20	62.21	70.45
	(b) Medium/Long term Loans	38.61	30.97	16.15	19.38
7.	Loans Recovered (Total)	78.14	–	59.94	67.72
	(a) Short-term	63.67	–	49.13	54.36
	(b) Medium/Long term	14.47	–	10.81	13.36
8.	Loans outstanding	188.33	–	116.09	132.65
	(a) Short term	144.94	–	75.65	86.14
	(b) Medium term	43.39	–	40.44	46.51

(Table Contd.)

Table (Contd...)

Sl. No.	Particulars	1985	1989	1994	1995
9.	Overdues	85.00	–	60.76	76.01
	(a) Short term	58.42	–	41.60	53.80
	(b) Medium/Long term	26.58	–	19.16	22.21
10.	Non-Credit Business (Total)	45.45	–	130.44	118.16
	(a) Produce Marketed	6.85	–	10.17	10.42
	(b) Goods Processed	0.01	–	23.65	–
	(c) Farm Requisites supplied	27.06	–	50.55	59.16
	(d) Consumer Goods Sold	11.53	–	46.07	48.58
11.	Government Aid Received (Total)	5.12	–	4.18	9.93
	(a) Loans	1.84	–	1.01	0.94
	(b) Subsidy	3.28	–	3.17	8.99
12.	No. of Godowns				
	(a) Owned	2688	–	1910	1935
	(b) Hired	1292	–	686	587
13.	No. of Societies at profit/loss				
	(a) At profit	1419	–	862	813
	(b) At loss	1168	–	1358	1415
	(c) Without profit or loss	251	–	91	79

Source: Statistical statements relating to the Co-operative Movement in India, part-1, Credit Societies, NABARD, 1987, 1991, 1996 and 1997, pp. 331-337.

crores in 1994, but have increased to Rs. 132.65 crores in 1995. The same tendency can be seen with regard to overdues. Processing activity has shown volatility in the selected years. It was of the value of just Rs. 0.01 crores in 1985 which increased to Rs. 23.65 crores in 1994.

Table 2.5 shows cost of management in lamps which includes mainly salaries, rent and depreciation.

Procurement and Sale of Minor Forest Produce by LAMPS

.ne major activity of the Large-sized Adivasi Multipurpose Co-operative Societies is supposed to be procurement and sale of minor forest produce (MFP), also called Non-Timber Forest Produce (NTFP), or Non-wood Forest Produce (NWFP). Since wood and timber are considered major forest products, other produces of forest origin which can be easily extracted and which are of commercial and medicinal value, have been considered minor forest produces. It is viewed that prominent minor forest produces are about 30 in number which are available for extraction and marketing. Apart from these there are hundreds of medicinal herbs which are also considered minor forest products. Minor forest produce, generally includes, bamboo, mineral, plant and animal products other than timber and fuel wood. Some important minor forest produces which have become part and parcel of tribal life are honey, tamarind, Amla (Emblica Officinalis), Antwala (Sapindus emarginatus) tree mass, Soapnut, Gum Karaya (Sterculila Urens), Niger seed (Guizotia abyssinica), Myrobalan, Soyabean, Lac, Cardamom, Turmeric, Dalchinni, Mahuwa-Flower, Sal Seed, Puwad Seed, Deer Antler, leaves and flowers. Many oil seeds have also found place as minor forest produces.

Table 2.5

Cost of Management in LAMPS-1995

(Rs. in Lakhs)

Sl. No.	*State/Union Territory*	*Salaries*	*Rent paid*	*Depreciation*	*Other expenses*	*Total*
1.	Arunachal Pradesh	NA	NA	NA	NA	NA
2.	Assam	NA	NA	NA	NA	NA
3.	Bihar	36.68	2.38	0.19	96.15	135.40
4.	Dadra and Nagar Haveli	3.48	0.06	0.30	3.23	7.07
5.	Daman and Diu	3.41	0.08	0.35	0.70	4.54
6.	Gujarat	80.06	6.03	32.14	209.19	327.42
7.	Karnataka	19.40	0.68	5.86	9.34	35.28
8.	Madhya Pradesh	NA	NA	NA	NA	NA
9.	Maharashtra	55.51	8.08	1.15	103.17	167.91
10.	Manipur	NA	NA	NA	NA	NA
11.	Mizoram	NA	NA	NA	NA	NA
12.	Nagaland	NA	NA	NA	NA	NA
13.	Orissa	275.33	1.80	2.10	186.96	466.19
14.	Rajasthan	63.31	3.51	1.16	43.82	111.80
15.	Tamil Nadu	9.74	2.13	7.56	6.05	25.48
16.	Tripura	47.80	0.61	9.21	10.29	67.91

Source: Statistical statements relating to the co-operative movement in India, 1994-95, NABARD, 1997, p. 336.

Collection and marketing of minor forest produce is the major income generating activity undertaken by LAMPS. Though there has been much diversification in the activities of LAMPS in subsequent years, the main aim with which they were organised was to collect different minor forest produces from their tribal members and to market them as a commercial venture.

Since each LAMPS has a jurisdiction of one block/ Tehsil or a certain area, it can extract minor forest produces from that particular area. But the forest belongs to the forest department. Hence the LAMPS has to get the forest area on lease for certain period on payment of royalty to the forest department. Lease period will be usually two years, after the expiry of which the LAMPS has to again apply to the forest department for a fresh lease. The Task Force on Development of Tribal Areas (1973) of the planning commission[17] had indicated that the permit system for collection of raw materials should be abolished and tribals be allowed to collect minor forest produce free of charge. Since LAMPS are organised to serve the purposes of tribal members and have to run on an operative profit basis, it can be widely accepted that they have to get the forest area on lease and be permitted by the government, i.e., forest department, who is the real owner of the forest wealth. Lease money paid to the forest department works as one of the cost items to the society and while fixing the profit margin in the sale of minor forest produces, this cost factor is amply taken account of.

Management of LAMPS

Uniqueness of LAMPS is that it is a society administered and managed largely by tribal people. Tribals dominate the board of directors, i.e., the administrative body of the society. The LAMPS works under the control and authority of this board of directors elected or constituted by the members of the society under the byelaws framed for this purpose.

Constitution of the board of directors of LAMPS varies from state to state. Normally it consists of nine to thirteen directors. Out of this total number, a majority will be elected directors and a handful are ex-officio or nominated directors i.e., nominated by the government. These ex-officio directors are officers of different government departments which have to work in close co-ordination with tribal people and tribal organisations. These officers are usually Assistant Registrar of Co-operative Societies, Tahsildar, Block Development Officer, Social Welfare Officer, and officer belonging to integrated tribal development project, representative from the financing bank, i.e., district central co-operative bank etc., In general, two to three officers above mentioned and in some cases even upto five officers will be on the board of directors of LAMPS. In Karnataka State the Co-operative Societies Act as amended in 1998 restricts the number of directors to nine for a society having jurisdiction of less than a taluka, to eleven directors for a society having jurisdiction upto a taluka, and to thirteen directors if the jurisdiction of the society extends beyond a taluka. Since most of the LAMPS in the state have tehsil (taluka) as their area of operation, the society has eleven directors on the board, six to nine being elected, and the remaining ex-officio.

In the states where persons belonging to scheduled caste are enrolled as members, each LAMPS includes one or two directors on its board belonging to this community. But they are barred from holding the office of Chairman or Vice-Chairman of the society. The Chairman and Vice-Chairman of these societies shall be invariably from scheduled tribes.

In Karnataka and Daman and Diu where persons belonging to only scheduled tribes are enrolled as members of LAMPS, all the elected directors will be from the scheduled tribes category.

A Brief Review of the Working of LAMPS in Different States

What follows is a brief review of the system of working of LAMPS in different states of India.

Madhya Pradesh impockets largest tribal population among all Indian states. Hence the relevance of LAMPS in Madhya Pradesh is immense. The tribal sub-plan was first introduced in Madhya Pradesh in 1974-75 and the LAMPS came into being with this scheme in the form of tribal service societies. Out of the 689 LAMPS in the State as in 1995, 19 have been organised at block level and the remaining 670 at 'hat' (market) level amalgamating in all 2639 primary societies. Out of the covered districts four are fully tribal districts, namely, Bastar, Mandala, Jhabua and Sarguja. In eleven districts more than half of their areas is under tribal sub-plan and they are also treated as tribal districts. 384 LAMPS are newly formed in the State, and the total number of these institutions as in March 1998 stands at 1,073.

The LAMPS are linked with central co-operative banks for their credit and with regional marketing societies established at Raipur, Bilaspur, Jabalpur and Indore for their marketing operations. They have close links also with land development banks in the field of long-term credit supply. To safeguard the tribals from vested interests and to ensure a fair representation of tribal people on the management, two-third seats in the board of directors have been reserved for scheduled tribes in all LAMPS. If any society fails to elect the members of the board, the Registrar of co-operative societies shall nominate the members of the board from amongst the eligible tribal members.

LAMPS in Jagdalpur and Bastar areas of Madhya Pradesh State have been doing a commendable job. The mainstay of the tribal economy in these areas is minor forest produces such as tamarind, honey and mahua. The practice was that the tribals would collect these produces from the forests and sell them at towns after some sort of processing. The traders from the towns would buy these produces from the tribals at low prices and on unjustified terms. In the process, tribal earned less than 20 percent of the final price of the produce whereas the trader and mandi merchant earned exorbitantly. The money lender and the trader used to procure tamarind for as low as Rs. 2 per kg. which he could sell at a ready market in Jagdalpur for Rs. 10 per kg. It has been estimated that tribals were losing Rs. 200 crores annually due to malpractices indulged in by traders.

LAMPS handled tamarind business on a very large scale in 1998-99 and TRIFED was gracious enough to lend a helping hand in this venture by directly purchasing the produce from LAMPS. These societies procured about 8,000 quintal of tamarind in that year and the tribal collector got Rs. 8 per kg.

Tribal sub-plan was introduced in Maharashtra State in 1976. To ensure provision of credit and marketing facilities to tribals and thereby to bring about their economic welfare the state Government took the decision of creating one LAMP society for every 12,500 population. Accordingly, 275 LAMPS were established in 15 districts of the State between 1976 and 1983. Taking an objective view that LAMPS are the real centres through which the tribal development programmes could be speedily implemented, the State Government started providing huge amount of finances to these societies.

A number of regulations and legal enactments were framed by the State Government to protect the tribals from exploitation. Of special importance is an act called "The

Maharashtra Tribal Economic Condition (Improvement) Act" which was enacted in 1976 as an anti-exploitative measure. The Act, among other things, envisages prohibition of lending by private agencies, marketing of certain agricultural and minor forest produces in tribal areas by any other agencies except those notified by the State Government from time to time. The Maharashtra State Co-operative Tribal Development Corporation was established in 1972 and it has been appointed as the chief agent of the Government to implement monopoly procurement scheme as envisaged in the Act of 1976.

But the LAMPS in Maharashtra State did not fare well. By 1982, about 230 LAMPS out of 275 were working under heavy losses, and recovery of loans from members registered less than 30 percent. Total losses of all LAMPS was of the order of about Rs. 400 Lakhs. The State Government appointed a Committee headed by Madhokar Rao Pichad to study the situation and to make necessary recommendations. The committee popularly known as "Pichad Committee" which submitted its report in 1983 observed that LAMPS had failed to sustain themselves owing to lack of foresight and effective financial management. As per the recommendations of this committee, LAMPS were divided into smaller "Tribal Development and Service Co-operative Societies". Each LAMPS was divided into three to four societies, each covering 5,000 tribal population and having jurisdiction over 8 to 10 kilometres. Accordingly, 938 societies of smaller size were set up in all the tribal sub-plan areas. Though the LAMPS were divided into smaller units, their objectives and functions remained the same, only their geographical jurisdiction was narrowed down.

LAMPS are members of the Maharashtra State Co-operative Tribal Development Corporation, a federal organisation undertaking monopoly procurement of minor forest produces. The corporation is head quartered at Nasik. As suggested by the Pichad Committee, employees of all LAMPS were taken on the staff of the Corporation.

LAMPS in Maharashtra are at present popularly called "Adivasi Co-operative Societies-ACS" also known as "Adivasi Vividh Sahakari Samstha Societies'. There are 984 such societies in the State at present. Being members of the State Co-operative Tribal Development Corporation, these societies are working as its agents in procurement of minor forest produce and surplus agricultural produce and also for routing consumption finance to members. The society purchases minor forest produces and surplus agricultural produce (SAP) from the members and sells them to the TDC which is the chief agent of the State Government.

In Bihar, LAMPS are working as Procurement agents of State Co-operative Tribal Development Corporation, and Tribal Co-operative Marketing Development Federation (TRIFED) hires the services of LAMPS in a bigway to procure minor forest produces. Government patronage to LAMPS has been in many ways such as loans, subsidy and share capital. But unfortunately a majority of the LAMPS in the state are working under loss and they are not in a position to muster funds to carry on the business. Since many of the LAMPS are in the red and not in a position to procure minor forest produces, Primary Agricultural Co-operative Societies also called Vyapara Mandals do the business of procurement and sale of minor forest and surplus agricultural produces.

But State Co-operative Tribal Development Corporation in Bihar is almost defunct. It is not in a condition to procure and market minor forest produces on a large scale.

In Rajastan, LAMPS undertake procurement and sale of minor forest produces as their main business. They also undertake public distribution of essential commodities and also sale of fertilisers. LAMPS are members of the Rajasthan Tribal Area Development Co-operative Federation, a federal agency created by the State Government to undertake procurement and sale of minor forest produces and to implement tribal development measures. This federation purchases minor forest produces from LAMPS and sells them to the TRIFED and also in the open market. LAMPS have been getting huge amount of funds in the form of loans, subsidy and share capital by the government.

In Gujarat LAMPS exist, but their activities are very limited. They have not undertaken the business of procuring and selling minor forest produce. Instead, they procure pulses and other surplus agricultural produces and sell them to TRIFED and in the open market. Thus, LAMPS act as agents of TRIFED in procurement of surplus agricultural produce.

But the LAMPS do not have pooling centres or collection centres of their own. Hence, premises of agricultural produce marketing committees have been made market places where the authorities of LAMPS purchase surplus agricultural produce from tribals. LAMPS give publicity about the prices of different produces and other details in order to make the marketing convenient.

It has been found that majority of the LAMPS in Gujarat are earning an operative profit and have been serving the tribals in different ways. They sell consumer goods and agricultural inputs, and some of the LAMPS have undertaken loaning operations.

Since LAMPS do not have the right to procure MFPs, that business is handled by the Gujarat State Forest Development Corporation. The Corporation was established in 1976 under the Companies Act of 1956 with an initial authorised capital of Rs. 1 crore. It is head quartered at Baroda. Trade of MFP was in the hands of private Contractors who used to exploit tribals by various means before the entry of the Corporation into this field. The corporation, therefore took up the activity of MFP collection and marketing since the beginning as this has a considerable bearing on the tribal economy. Only three MFPs such as Timru leaves, Doli and Mahuwa flowers were collected by the Corporation in 1976 which has now gone upto 55 commodities. Collection of many minor forest produces has been nationalised by the Government of Gujarat under the Gujarat Minor Forest Produce Trade Nationalisation Act 1979, and sole collection rights are given to the Corporation. It collects MFPs through its branches directly from the tribals.

Orissa is another state which has a large chunk of tribal population. The tribal sub-plan in the State consists of 118 blocks predominated with tribal population. These blocks are in the districts of Mayurbhanj, Keonjhar, Sundargarh, Koraput, Phulbani, Ganjam, Kalahandi, Sambalpur and Balasore. As per the recommendations of the Bawa Committee, LAMPS were organised in the State since 1976-77. Before formation of LAMPS there were in existence service co-operative societies which undertook provision of short and medium term loan, paddy loan and distribution of fertiliser. In a majority of the cases the existing service co-operative societies were converted into LAMPS by amending their bye-laws enblock to make provision for them to take up all the functions the LAMPS were supposed to undertake, and the area of operation was also extended. In some cases a few LAMPS were newly created. In cases where another service co-operative society was functioning in the area of operation of the newly formed LAMPS, such society was kept under suspended animation and was later liquidated or amalgamated. In view of larger areas of operation and with a view to provide better services to tribals, many LAMPS have branches in their area of operation. In many cases the services of the Secretary and the Staff of the then Service Co-operative Society were taken over by the LAMPS. There are at present 223 LAMPS in existence in the State.

Government's assistance to LAMPS will be usually of three types, viz., loan, subsidy and share capital. In the beginning the Government had doled out Rs. 25,000/- as managerial subsidy to each LAMPS.

LAMPS function as agents of the State Co-operative Tribal Development Corporation whose main function is to procure and sell minor forest produces.

But the performance of LAMPS in Orissa State is dismal indeed. Only 2 out of 223 LAMPS were working on an operative profit at the end of financial year 1999!

But the most unfortunate thing is that much help has not come to LAMPS from the State Tribal Development Corporation. Linkage between the LAMPS and the TDC is not on the expected lines. TDC fears to advance money to LAMPS for procurement of produce and in turn tribals are, by and large, unaware of the existence of TDC. The horrible scenario is tribals sell away MFP and surplus agricultural produces to private traders at a very low price. It is a pity that the TDC and the LAMPS have failed to avoid distress sales.

There are 11 LAMPS in the State of Tamil Nadu. But almost all LAMPS in the State are working under losses. Potentiality for minor forest produces in Tamil Nadu is very high since the State has large pockets of hill and forest areas. But the role of LAMPS in procurement and marketing of minor forest produces is only nominal. The reason for this is that LAMPS show keen interest in other tribal welfare activities enunciated in the tribal sub-plan strategy such as providing Jewel loans and animal husbandry loans to tribal people.

Only some LAMPS in Tamil Nadu are engaged in the business of extraction and sale of minor forest produce. The state forest department every year fixes auctions to lease out forest land for collection of MFP. LAMPS participate in the public auction to get the lease. The prominent reasons for many of the LAMPS not taking part in public auction to get the lease are fixation of a very high amount of lease by the forest department and lack of necessary funds with the LAMPS. Thus, a large quantity of minor forest produces is purchased by private traders at a very low price.

In Tamil Nadu, Tribal Co-operative Marketing Development Federation has been doing a wonderful job in purchasing MFP from LAMPS. TRIFED and LAMPS have developed a very good business contact in the sphere of collection and sale of MFP. TRIFED usually collects from LAMPS commodities such as tamarind, soapnut, gallnut and hillgrass. Though LAMPS are collecting honey, TRIFED has not yet ventured to purchase this commodity from LAMPS. TRIFED in Tamil Nadu has embarked upon this commercial activity of procurement of minor forest produces from LAMPS in the last four years.

In the north-eastern region, LAMPS are in existence only in six states, such as, Arunachal Pradesh, Assam, Manipur, Mizoram, Nagaland and Tripura. In other words, among the north-eastern states, Meghalaya has no LAMPS. In this region of India, many types of tribal co-operative societies such as LAMPS, primary agricultural co-operative societies and primary marketing societies are in existence. Thus, LAMPS are just one type of tribal societies in that part of the country. LAMPS in these states undertake the activities of collection and sale of minor forest produces and distribution of consumer articles.

Twenty one LAMPS are in existence in Karnataka State. Some of these societies were established in the state starting from the year 1965 which were then called 'Forest Labour Contract Societies'. With the implementation of tribal sub-plan strategy, more and more number of societies were organised in the latter part of 1970s. Forest labour contract societies wherever they were in existence were converted into LAMPS. A special feature in the organisation of LAMPS in Karnataka is that twenty of these societies have been organised only in Mysore division, only where the integrated tribal development plan is in operation. Only one LAMPS is in existence in Bhatkal of North Canara district of Belgaum division.

The most important activity LAMPS have undertaken in Karnataka is procurement and sale of minor forest produces. They are engaged in other activities also such as distribution of essential commodities under public distribution system, sale of consumer articles and agricultural inputs and supply of food grains and consumer articles to hostels. A few LAMPS have embraced banking activity also. They accept different types of deposits and advance loans under a number of schemes.

As at the end of the financial year 2002 LAMPS in Karnataka had a total membership of 62,639 and a share capital of Rs. 236.44 Lakhs. Fourteen societies had an accumulated profit and the remaining Seven societies were working under accumulated losses as on 31.3.2001.

State LAMPS Federation has been established in Karnataka in the year 1998. This is the first ever such federation in the whole of India. This federation is headquartered at Mysore.

The Tribal Co-operative Marketing Development Federation-Trifed

In the spheres of tribal development, minor forest produces business and activities of LAMPS, the role of

Tribal Co-operative Marketing Development Federation-TRIFED, finds a special and an important place. TRIFED has been set up by the Government of India to pay specific attention to the marketing requirements of tribal forest and agricultural produce and to help speed up the process of assimilation of tribals into the economic main stream of the country. It came into existence in 1987 and is head quartered at New Delhi.

TRIFED is an apex level federation of the State Tribal Development Co-operative Federations and the State Forest Corporations. It has its own national network for procurement, processing and marketing of forest and agricultural commodities produced in the tribal areas of the country. TRIFED has opened zonal offices at Mumbai and Guwahati and Regional Offices at Nasik, Ahmedabad, Udaipur, Jagdalpur, Bhopal, Chennai, Hyderabad, Bangalore, Bhubaneswar, Ranchi and Calcutta.

TRIFED like any other co-operative institution has adopted bye laws for governance. Its broad objectives are full utilisation of natural produce of the tribal areas by improving their marketability, ensuring higher earnings and employment opportunities for the tribes, creation of awareness of market forces among the tribal people, enabling them to optimise their incomes and lending marketing support to state tribal co-operative Federations and Forest Corporations engaged in procurement and sale of agricultural and minor forest produces.

TRIFED procures and markets over 50 items of forest and agricultural produces including spices, dry fruits, oil seeds, medicinal herbs and processed foods. Since most of the tribal areas are remote regions and are not accessible even by road, TRIFED has set up hundreds of procurement centres all over the country. To ensure that the produce is not only collected fresh but also stays that way, a chain of warehouses and refrigerated storage facilities are established at strategic locations. The Federation has ensured quality control of the highest international standards. For this, it has set up two well-equipped research and development laboratories at Delhi and Jagdalpur.

TRIFED is engaged also in exports of about 20 minor forest produces in a very big way, important of which are Gum Karaya, Cashew nuts, Niger seed and Tendu leaves. It is making a breakthrough in procurement and marketing of rare medicinal plants and herbs.

A remarkable achievement of TRIFED is that it has set up plantations of commercial crops and industries based on tribal produce. Tribal industrial complexes are established in Madhya Pradesh, Gujarath, Rajasthan, Orissa, Bihar, West Bengal and Meghalaya. These complexes are entrusted with the responsibility of processing tribal produce which helps in adding value to these commodities.

As said earlier, TRIFED is an apex level institution co-ordinating the activities of state level federations and corporations engaged in procurement and sale of tribal produce. In the way it has been giving a fillip to the activities of LAMPS and has helped them undertake MFP business on a large scale. Minor forest produce and surplus agricultural produce collected by LAMPS are purchased by State level Federations and Corporations. These institutions sell them to TRIFED, which in turn sells them in the market in India and in other countries across the globe.

"TRIFED was thought of as a customary agent of change. The results of this have been quite evident. TRIFED's intervention helped in checking the malpractice of short weighing and unfair bartering, generating substantial employment for them, and boosting the ruling price of tribal produces".[18] TRIFED has come a long way towards improving the lot of indigenous people, those dependent upon forest produce for their livelihood, by providing them with remunerative prices for their products on the one hand and generating large number of employment opportunities on the other. Its efforts in the field of tribal service are laudable.

The Role of Girijan Co-operative Corporation in Tribal Development

The role of Girijan Co-operative Corporation (GCC), Andhra Pradesh, needs a special mention in the context of forest based tribal activity and tribal development. It is very interesting to note that though Andhra Pradesh is an abode of 33 scheduled tribes groups forming seven percent of the total population, LAMPS are not in existence in that State. Instead, GCC is dealing in the minor forest produces business.

In order to put and end to exploitation of tribal community by emancipating them from the clutches of private traders and to ensure a reasonable price for MFP, the State Government set up the Andhrapradesh Scheduled Tribes Finance and Development Corporation with head-quarters at Vishakapatnam in 1957. It was renamed as Girijan Co-operative Corporation in 1970.

The main marketing activities of GCC are purchase of MFP and agricultural produce and sale of domestic requirements to the tribals at fair prices. The following are the main functional objectives of the Corporation.

(i) To purchase MFP outright on monopoly basis from the tribals at fair prices,

(ii) To supply all daily requirements to the tribals through Daily Requirement Depots at cheaper rates,

(iii) To meet the credit requirements of tribal agriculturists,

(iv) To diversify the earnings of the tribals and supplement their income through some industrial units, and

(v) To implement welfare schemes for economic upliftment of tribals.

The Girijan Co-operative Corporation has a network of one regional office at Hyderabad and 12 Divisional Offices in different parts of the State, its affiliated 45 Girijan Primary Co-operative Marketing Societies (GPCMS), and their 817 DR Depots.

GCC procures MFP and agricultural produce through its daily requirement Depots. These Depots purchase the commodities directly from tribal people. Thus DR Depots are doing the business as LAMPS do in other states. These depots serve as branches of GCC for purchase and sale of produce and have been established even in remote areas. Price of MFP to be offered to the tribals is fixed by a committee constituted by the State Government.

Earlier GPCMS were working as branches of GCC. But since 1970 the GCC has started advancing loans to tribals and this activity is being performed through GPCMS. For this purpose GPCMS have been registered under Co-operative Societies Act. GCC advances term loans to tribals at a rate of interest of 12 percent and it is recovered out of sales of the produce. Recovery of loans is to the extent of about 70 percent.

At present GCC has 2433 employees who are engaged in the service of two million tribals. The corporation is doing a marvellous job in the field of tribal development.

Main Finding in the Chapter

Large-sized Adivasi Multi-purpose Co-operative Societies have been in existence in 16 states and two union territories of India. They have been organised to provide all possible types of assistance to the tribal population which is a neglected lot. LAMPS have been established in India mainly with governmental intervention and the largesse doled out by it. Though it was visualised to organise one LAMPS in each block or tehsil, in many states such as Maharashtra and Orissa, each block has 3 or 4 LAMPS in it. In many states LAMPS have been formed or restructured to suit local needs.

Uniformity in organisational structure and area of operation of LAMPS is lacking. It is different in different states and union territories. Seen from the business point of view, collection and sale of minor forest produces and surplus agricultural produces is the major activity in majority of the LAMPS. But in Karnataka, LAMPS have not so far undertaken the surplus agricultural produces business. In Gujarat, LAMPS have not been permitted to take up MFP activity. A large number of LAMPS in all states and union territories where they exist, have undertaken public distribution of rationed goods as well as sale of consumer goods and agricultural inputs.

Though LAMPS were expected to bring about tribal welfare by catering to the needs of that section of population, performance of these societies in many states over half a century of their existence is dismal indeed. A huge number of LAMPS are working under heavy losses, many of the LAMPS are under the mercy of traders and middlemen to market the produce they collect and a large number of LAMPS are not in a position to contribute their mite to the well-being of their members. But there is a ray of hope also. A good number of LAMPS have shown their worth, accomplished their purpose and have been able to take up a large number of activities so as to help the members in a number of ways.

REFERENCES

1. Government of India, *Report of the National Commission on Agriculture,* 1976, p. 149.

2. Ibid.,

3. Government of India, *Summary Report of the Study Team on Co-operative Structure in Tribal Development Agency Projects,* 1973, p.1.

4. Ibid.

5. Guru, H.N.-*"Tribal Co-operatives in Madhya Pradesh The LAMPS",* The Co-operator, April 15, 1984.

6. Government of India, *Summary Report of the Study Team on Co-operatives Structure in Tribal Development Agency Projects,* 1973, p.2.

7. Ibid., p. 3.

8. Sharachchandra Lele and R. Jagannath Rao, *"Whose Co-operatives and whose Produce? The case of LAMPS in Karnataka"* in the Book 'Rediscovering Co-operation' (Ed.) by R. Rajagopalan, Institute of Rural Development Anand, 1996, p. 55-56.

9. Ibid, p. 55.

10. Government of India, Ministry of Home Affairs, New Delhi, *Census of India, 1991,* Statement 1, p. XII.

11. Ibid, Series-1, List of Scheduled Castes and Scheduled Tribes.

12. Government of India, *Report of the National Commission on Agriculture,* 1976, p. 151.

13. Ibid., p. 147.

14. Dr. B.K. Roy Burman, *Issues in Tribal Development* (Unpublished paper).

15. Sarveshwara Rao and G. Parthasarathy (Ed.), *Regulated Markets and Public Policy,* Institute of Development and Planning Studies, Vishakapatnam, 1995, p. 49.

16. Bhupinder Singh, *"The Tribal Problem-Some Reflections"* (Unpublished paper).

17. Government of India, *Report of the National Commission on Agriculture,* 1976, pp. 151-152.

18. Sanjay Kumar Verma, *"Coops: Harbinger of Change in Bastar",* The Co-operator, July 1999.

CHAPTER — 3

Progress of LAMPS in Karnataka-A Quantitative and Qualitative Assessment

An attempt to provide a bird's eye view of the structure and working of LAMPS in India had been made in the previous chapter. A study of the organisation and functioning of LAMPS in Karnataka State, their success as well as failures, and causes thereto, and their quantitative and qualitative performance over the years has been undertaken in the present chapter . A glimpse of Karnataka LAMPS Federation which has been established of late, and which is first of its kind in the entire country has been provided at the end of the chapter.

What follows is a quantitative and qualitative assessment of the working of LAMPS in Karnataka. Important quantitative parameters are growth of membership, volume of business handled, accumulated profit enjoyed, or loss suffered by LAMPS. Main qualitative parameters used are service of LAMPS to members and social and ecological performance of LAMPS.

There are at present twenty one Large-sized Adivasi Multipurpose co-operative societies in existence in

Karnataka state. Twenty of these societies are situated across seven districts of Mysore division which consists of eight districts. One LAMPS is situated in North Kanara district of Belgaum division. District wise number of LAMPS in existence is Mysore-2, Chamarajanagar-4, Coorg-3, Chikmagalur-2, Mangalore-5, Udupi-3, Mandya-1 and North Canara-1.

In Karnataka, the first LAMPS was organised at Heggadadevana Kote of Mysore district in 1965. Two more LAMPS were established in the year 1967, one at B.R. Hills of erstwhile Mysore district and the other at Puttur in South Kanara district. In the beginning these institutions were called Forest Labour Co-Operative Societies or Labour Contract Multi-Purpose Societies. Some more LAMPS were established in some other districts of Mysore division in subsequent years.

These societies in Karnataka were organised as part of tribal sub-plan programme as in other states of India. According to the new norm adopted by the Government of India of taking up of an area for special treatment by forming integrated tribal development project if that area impockets scheduled tribes population of more than ten thousand, the districts of Mysore, Coorg, South Kanara and Chikmagalur were considered ITDP areas. With the adoption of this approach in 1974-75, a number of LAMPS were organised in subsequent years and the Labour contract Multi-Purpose Societies or Forest Labour Co-operative Societies existed till then were converted into and renamed as LAMPS. Thus, 20 LAMPS have been established till date in ITDP area and one LAMPS i.e., at Muthathi in Mandya district has been formed outside that area. The basic reason for organising this LAMPS even though it falls outside ITDP area is that it has a concentration of 115 tribal families which have nothing to fall back upon for livelihood except MFP collection. The area is rich with tamarind trees and with honey. It was thought of by the authorities that formation of a society to collect and market MFP in the area might help the tribal people.

The name of the LAMPS, the district in which it is situated and the date and year of its establishment are shown in the following table.

Table 3.1

Name of the LAMPS, the District and the Date of Establishment

Sl. No.	*Name of the LAMPS*	*District*	*Date of Establishment*
1.	LAMPS Hunsur	Mysore	24.03.1971
2.	LAMPS Heggadadevanakote	Mysore	30.12.1976
3.	LAMPS Chamarajanagar	Chamarajanagar	20.11.1978
4.	LAMPS Gundlupet	-do-	04.08.1982
5.	LAMPS B.R. Hills	-do-	17.03.1967
6.	LAMPS Hanur	-do-	04.12.1982
7.	LAMPS Thithimathi	Coorg	18.12.1976
8.	LAMPS Basavanahalli	-do-	17.01.1979
9.	LAMPS Bhagamandala	-do-	09.09.1982
10.	LAMPS Koppa	Chikmagalur	28.02.1979
11.	LAMPS Mudigere	-do-	28.02.1979
12.	LAMPS Suliys	Mangalore	17.02.1981
13.	LAMPS Puttur	-do-	23.03.1967
14.	LAMPS Bantwala	-do-	24.01.1983
15.	LAMPS Mangalore	-do-	05.08.1982
16.	LAMPS Belthangadi	-do-	12.01.1979
17.	LAMP Karkala	Udupi	04.09.1977
18.	LAMPS Kundapura	-do-	30.06.1983
19.	LAMPS Udupi	-do-	23.02.1977
20.	LAMPS Muthathi	Mandya	04.03.1994
21.	LAMPS Bhatkal	North Kanara	24.03.1994

Source: Data personally collected from the Societies.

The area of operation of each LAMPS in the state is by and large a taluka. But there are a few exceptions. The jurisdiction of some LAMPS covers more than one taluka. For example the area of operation of Hunsur LAMPS is Hunsur and Periyapatna talukas, of Koppa LAMPS is Koppa, Sringeri and Narasimharajapura talukas and of Mudigere LAMPS is Mudigere, Chikmagalur and Kadur talukas.

The area of operation of each LAMPS and the talukas over which it has jurisdiction is indicated in the following table.

Table 3.2

Lamps and their area of operation

Sl. NO.	*Name of the LAMPS*	*Jurisdictions*	*Name of the taluka*
1.	LAMPS Hunsur	Two talukas	Hunsur Periyapatna
2.	LAMPS Heggadadevanakote	One taluka	Heggad-adevanakote
3.	LAMPS Chamarajanagar	One taluka	Chamaraj-anagar
4.	LAMPS Gundlupet	One taluka	Gundlupet
5.	LAMPS B.R. Hills	One taluka	Yalandur
6.	LAMPS Hanur	One taluka	Kollegal
7.	LAMPS Thithimathi	One taluka	Virajpet
8.	LAMPS Basavanahalli	One taluka	Somawarpet
9.	LAMPS Bhagamandala	One taluka	Madjkeri
10.	LAMPS Koppa	Three talukas	Koppa Sringeri Narasimhar-ajapura
11.	LAMPS Mudigere	Three talukas	Mudigere Chikmagalur Kadur

(Table Contd.)

(Table Contd.)

Sl. NO.	*Name of the LAMPS*	*Jurisdictions*	*Name of the taluka*
12.	LAMPS Sullia	One taluka	Sulia
13.	LAMPS Puttur	One taluka	Puttur
14.	LAMPS Bantwala	One taluka	Bantwala
15.	LAMPS Mangalore	One taluka	Mangalore
16.	LAMPS Belthangadi	One taluka	Belthangadi
17.	LAMPS Karkala	One taluka	Karkala
18.	LAMPS Kundapura	One taluka	Kundapura
19.	LAMPS Udupi	One taluka	Udupi
20.	LAMPS Muthathi	One taluka	Malavalli
21.	LAMPS Bhatkal	One taluka	Bhatkal

Source: Data personally collected from the Societies.

Table 3.2 amply indicates that except for three LAMPS i.e., Koppa, Mudigere and Hunsur, each of the remaining 18 LAMPS have only one taluka in their area of operation.

Again, except for five LAMPS, the remaining 16 LAMPS have their taluka centres as head quarters of the society. The five LAMPS which do not have taluka centres as their head quarters are Muthathi, B.R. Hills, Thithimati, Basavanahalli and Bhagamandala.

Over the years the number of LAMPS has increased, their membership enrolment has gone up, business of many LAMPS has registered voluminous growth and they have been able to diversify their activities.

Tribal population is of two types, viz; hill tribes and non-hill tribes. Some LAMPS have only non hill tribes as their members since the area in which the society is operating impockets only these tribes, whereas some societies have both hill tribes and non-hill tribes as their members.

Table 3.3 shows the tribal families covered by each LAMPS, number of members and share capital.

It is of interest to know the composition of hill tribes and non-hill tribes in the total membership of each LAMPS. In some LAMPS all the members belong to the hill tribes group whereas in some LAMPS there are only non-hill tribes members. But in some LAMPS there is a mixture of both the categories. The LAMPS which have only hill tribes as their members are Chamarajanagar, B.R. Hills, Hanur, Bhatkal, Thithimathi, Bhagamandala and Muthathi. The LAMPS in which all the members belong to the non-hill tribes category are Gundlupet, Koppa, Mudigere, Sullia, Puttur, Bantwala, Mangalore, Belthangadi, Kundapura and Udupi. In Hunsur, Heggadadevanakote, Basavanahalli and Karkala LAMPS, members belong to both hill tribes and non-hill tribes groups. Percentage of hill tribes and non-hill tribes members respectively in each of these LAMPS is about 30 and 70 in Hunsur LAMPS, about 90 and 10 in Heggadadevanakote LAMPS, about 25 and 75 in Basavanahalli LAMPS and about 50 and 50 in Karkala LAMPS.

The above analysis amply indicates that people belonging to non-hill tribes category predominate in the membership of LAMPS in Karnataka.

Altogether 21 LAMPS had a membership of 64,118 covering 44,430 tribal families. Hunsur LAMPS has the highest membership with 6421 and Muthathi LAMPS has the lowest membership with just 300. Tribal families residing in the area of operation of Muthathi LAMPS is also less with just 115.

Share capital assumes greater significance in that it helps the institution in increasing its working capital and thereby strengthens its resource base. It is also an indicator with regard to volume of membership and members' contribution to the funds of the society. As on

Table 3.3

Tribal Families, Membership and Share capital

Sl. No.	Name of the LAMPS	Tribal Families	No. of Members as on 31.3.1999	Share Capital (Rs. in Lakhs		
				Members	Government	Total
1.	LAMPS Hunsur	2,467	6,421	2.29	10.80	13.09
2.	LAMPS Heggadadevanakote	4,152	4,456	0.98	7.20	8.18
3.	LAMPS Chamarajanagar	770	1,270	0.45	8.10	8.55
4.	LAMPS Gundlupet	679	1,701	0.17	6.33	6.50
5.	LAMPS B.R. Hills	405	865	0.70	13.69	14.39
6.	LAMPS Hanur	4,500	3,483	0.40	10.13	10.53
7.	LAMPS Thithimathi	4,030	4,351	0.77	6.89	7.65
8.	LAMPS Basavanahalli	1,600	2,988	2.07	11.00	13.07
9.	LAMPS Bhagamandala	920	2,383	0.94	5.20	6.14
10.	LAMPS Koppa	1,565	2,702	2.69	21.95	24.64

(Table Contd.)

(Table Contd....)

Sl. No.	*Name of the LAMPS*	*Tribal Families*	*No. of Members as on 31.3.1999*	*Share Capital (Rs. in Lakhs*		
				Members	*Government*	*Total*
11.	LAMPS Mudigere	1,334	4,330	2.85	11.10	13.95
12.	LAMPS Sullia	1,877	2,657	0.71	14.13	14.84
13.	LAMPS Puttur	1,843	3.544	1.30	17.23	18.53
14.	LAMPS Bantwala	2,807	3,190	1.35	10.84	12.19
15.	LAMPS Mangalore	1,213	561	0.09	3.78	3.87
16.	LAMPS Belthangadi	2,253	4,264	0.59	6.48	7.07
17.	LAMPS Karkala	2,158	4,995	2.15	13.22	15.37
18.	LAMPS Kundapura	1,654	2,719	1.42	13.68	15.10
19.	LAMPS Udupi	5,088	5,459	2.29	20.33	22.62
20.	LAMPS Muthathi	115	300	0.15	–	0.15
21.	LAMPS Bhatkal	2,000	1479	8.43	4.83	13.26
	Total	**43,430**	**64,118**	**32.79**	**216.91**	**249.70**

Source: Data personally collected from the Societies.

31.3.1999 all the LAMPS put together had a share capital of Rs. 32.79 Lakhs. But the amount of members' share capital varies from LAMPS to LAMPS on a very large scale. Many LAMPS have not made attempts to collect share capital from their members by increasing the value of shares. For example, Gundlupet LAMPS with 1701 members could collect only Rs. 0.17 Lakhs, Hanur LAMPS with 3483 members could raise only Rs. 0.40 Lakhs and Mangalore LAMPS with 561 members could raise only Rs 0.09 lakhs as share capital. The average amount of share capital per each member works out to be Rs. 10 in Gundlupet LAMPS and a little above Rs. 10 in Hanur and Mangalore LAMPS.

As in other fields of co-operation, the Government has come forward in a big way in assisting the LAMPS in the form of share capital. Government's share capital is not given to Muthathi LAMPS. For the remaining 20 LAMPS, amount of share capital given by the state government has been Rs. 216.91 Lakhs. Out of the total share capital of Rs. 249.70 Lakhs of all the LAMPS as on 31.3.1999, Government's share with Rs. 216.91 Lakhs works out to be 87 per cent and members' share with Rs. 32.79 Lakhs works out to be just 13 per cent. This clearly indicates that LAMPS are at the mercy of the Government even to develop their resource base in the form of share capital. Government's share capital to LAMPS has been normally to admit members to the society and to strengthen working capital base of the institution.

Since tribals are vulnerable section of people both economically and socially it was the policy of the State Government to dole out funds in the form of membership share, admission fee and share fee to enrol members in the LAMPS. This policy was in vogue till 1996 and it was given up since then.

Growth of membership is one of the prominent quantitative indicators. As depicted in Table 3.4, total

Table 3.4
Growth of Membership

SI No.	Name of the LAMPS	1990-91	1992-93	1994-95	1996-97	1998-99
1.	LAMPS Hunsur	2025	2025	6421	6421	6421
2.	LAMPS Heggadadevanakote	2150	2246	3370	4205	4456
3.	LAMPS Chamarajanagar	706	710	955	1230	1270
4.	LAMPS gundlupet	1701	1701	1701	1701	1701
5.	LAMPS B.R. Hills	216	865	865	865	865
6.	LAMPS Hanur	2419	2419	2519	2950	3483
7.	LAMPS Thithimathi	4351	4351	4351	4351	4351
8.	LAMPS Basavanahalli	1671	2048	2890	2988	2988
9.	LAMPS Bhaamandala	2377	2393	2394	2895	2383
10.	LAMPS Koppa	1764	2294	2403	2648	2702

(Table Contd.)

(Table Contd....)

Sl No.	*Name of the LAMPS*	*1990-91*	*1992-93*	*1994-95*	*1996-97*	*1998-99*
11.	LAMPS Mudigere	2467	2644	3611	4269	4330
12.	LAMPS Sullia	1360	1944	2322	2558	2657
13.	LAMPS Puttur	2037	2262	2785	2918	3544
14.	LAMPS Bantwala	2208	2365	2676	2840	3190
15.	LAMPS Mangalore	113	113	419	544	561
16.	LAMPS Belthangadi	2640	3416	3900	4242	4264
17.	LAMPS Karkala	3093	3404	4425	4801	4995
18.	LAMPS Kundapura	1893	2019	2154	2690	2719
19.	LAMPS Udupi	3405	3546	4349	4867	5459
20.	LAMPS Muthathi	-	-	300	300	300
21.	LAMPS Bhatkal	-	-	-	-	1479
	Total	**38596**	**42765**	**64,118**	**60283**	**62639**

Source: Data personally collected from the societies.

membership in the LAMPS of Karnataka has grown from 38596 in 1990-91 to 64,118 in 1998-99.

But enrolment of members in many LAMPS is not satisfactory. For example, membership in Chamarajanagar LAMPS was 706 in 1990-91, and it has increased to just 1270 in 1998-99. Membership in Gundlupet LAMPS has been constant at 1701 between 1990-91 and 1998-99. Membership in B.R. Hills LAMPS also remained constant at 865 between 1992-93 and 1998-99. But it should be acknowledged that a few LAMPS such as of Hunsur, Koppa, Mudigere, Belthangadi and Udupi have made steady efforts in increasing the membership over the years.

Government Assistance to LAMPS

Unlike the traditional modes of co-operation developed from within, the modern co-operatives are introduced from outside with government assistance and supervision. These cooperatives, rarely developed as a result of the felt needs of the tribals. LAMPS are not an exception to this. Government's assistance to these institutions is being given not only in the form of share capital but also in the form of loan and subsidy. It is the general view of the government that unless sufficient funds are routed to the LAMPS in the form of loan, subsidy or share capital, it is not possible for the LAMPS to be established to attain the stage of self sustenance. Since these are the institutions which are in existence to look after the needs of the weak, neglected and the downtrodden, it is natural for the Government to come out with many schemes to provide a helping hand. Funds to LAMPS are also given out of centrally sponsored schemes and from National Co-operative Development Corporation.

Important schemes with which the government had assisted the LAMPS in different times are: (i) Subsidy to open retail sales outlets, (ii) loan to implement public distribution system, (iii) subsidy for collection of minor forest produces, (iv) subsidy to impart training in different vocations, (v) margin money assistance, (vi) loan for construction of godowns (vii) Goernment's share capital, (ix) managerial subsidy and (x) financial assistance for establishment of processing units.

The list is not exhaustive but only indicative. Governmental assistance in a number of ways is pumped into Large-sized Adivasi Multi-purpose Co-operative Societies. If the LAMPS make use of these funds effectively they can no doubt be able to diversify their activities and to serve the members in the best way.

LAMPS have received a huge amount of assistance from the Government in the form of share capital, loan and subsidy. This is amply clear from table 3.5. Till the end of March 1999 LAMPS had received governmental assistance to the tune of Rs. 459.60 Lakhs. Out of this total amount of assistance, share capital amounted to Rs. 216.94 Lakhs, loan amounted to Rs. 119.06 crores and subsidy amounted to 123.63 crores. In the total assistance to LAMPS percentage of these three works out to be 46.63, 26.18 and 26.19 respectively. This assistance has been given to them in different years since inception Hence, it is clear that government patronage in different forms has supported the LAMPS in their endeavour to sustain and grow.

The following schemes with an allocation of Rs. 55.00 Lakhs were proposed to be implemented during the annual plan period of 1999-2000.[1]

(i) Assistance from National Co-operative Development Corporation to weak co-operatives in tribal areas.

(ii) Share capital assistance to LAMPS for expansion and diversification of non-credit

Table 3.5

Government Assistance to LAMPS (Rs. in Lakhs)

Sl. No.	*Name of the LAMPS*	*Share Capital*	*Loan*	*Subsidy*	*Total*
1.	LAMPS Hunsur	10.80	5.00	6.88	22.68
2.	LAMPS Heggadadevanakote	7.23	10.75	4.65	22.60
3.	LAMPS Chamarajanagar	8.10	6.76	3.43	18.29
4.	LAMPS Gundlupet	6.33	8.63	4.15	19.11
5.	LAMPS B.R. Hills	13.69	4.66	1.57	19.92
6.	LAMPS Hanur	10.13	1.15	0.73	12.01
7.	LAMPS Thithimathi	6.89	2.18	10.12	19.19
8.	LAMPS Basavanahalli	11.00	6.10	30.05	47.15
9.	LAMPS Bhagamandala	5.20	3.56	6.35	15.11
10.	LAMPS Koppa	21.95	8.95	9.00	39.90
11.	LAMPS Mudigere	11.10	9.16	14.73	34.99

(Table Contd.)

(Table Contd....)

Sl. No.	Name of the LAMPS	Share Capital	Loan	Subsidy	Total
12.	LAMPS Sullia	14.13	15.17	6.25	35.55
13.	LAMPS Puttur	17.23	9.76	5.10	32.09
14.	LAMPS Bantwala	10.84	5.37	1.74	17.95
15.	LAMPS Mangalore	3.78	1.91	1.61	7.30
16.	LAMPS Belthangadi	6.48	3.88	5.86	16.22
17.	LAMPS Karkala	13.22	5.62	7.13	25.97
18.	LAMPS Kundapura	13.68	5.35	1.33	20.36
19.	LAMPS Udupi	20.33	5.10	1.95	27.38
20.	LAMPS Muthathi	–	–	1.00	1.00
21.	LAMPS Bhatkal	4.83	–	–	4.83
	Total	**216.94**	**119.06**	**123.63**	**459.60**

Source: Data personally collected from the societies.

business. This assistance from National Cooperative Development Corporation is to the extent of Rs. 2.00 Lakhs per society. This assistance is supposed to enable the LAMPS to enhance their borrowing power and thereby to take up different forms of non-credit business.

(iii) Financial assistance for establishment of processing units by LAMPS. This assistance is provided by the state Government to LAMPS to establish processing units of their own.

(iv) Subsidy to LAMPS for having basic amenities. Under this scheme assistance will be provided for basic amenities and marketing activities at the state level. This will enable the LAMPS to develop marketing facilities and to get out of the clutches of middlemen.

Structure and Management

Membership is open to all adult tribals living in the area of operation of the LAMPS. Board of Directors is the governing council of the society. Directors of the board are elected by members at the election fixed for the purpose. The LAMPS which has a taluka as its jurisdiction has 11 directors on the board. But uniformity with regard to the number of elected and ex-officio directors in the LAMPS of different districts is lacking. For example, in South Kanara and Udupi districts, of the 11 directors, 9 are elected from among tribals and the remaining 2 are ex-officio. In Mandya district, seven directors are elected and the remaining four are ex-officio. In Mysore, Chamarajanagar and Chikmagalur districts, of 11 directors, six are elected members from among tribals and five are ex-officio members : Range Forest officer, Tahsildar, Integrated Tribal Development Plan programme officer, Block Development officer and a nominee of the financing bank. In Coorg district, of the 11 directors, eight are elected from among tribals and the remaining three are ex-officio members. In other states where persons belonging to scheduled castes are also enrolled as members of LAMPS one or two directors of the board are from that Community. But in Karnataka, where membership in the LAMPS is restricted only to scheduled tribes, elected directors in the board will invariably be tribals.

Meetings of the board of directors are required to be conducted once in a month. Directors of the board elect the President who is an elected director. In other words, ex-officio directors are not expected to be elected or nominated as President. But there are a few exceptions. LAMPS of B.R. Hills has got Assistant Conservator of Forests as the President and of Chamarajanagar, Muthathi and Hunsur have Deputy Conservators of Forest of the locality as Presidents. This is against the principle ingrained in the model bye-law which ordains that only elected members can hold the post of President. But these LAMPS have allowed Assistant Conservator and Deputy Conservators who are ex-officio directors to be presidents.

President and Secretary are responsible for the day-to-day administration of the society. Financial powers are vested jointly in the President and Secretary.

General body of members is the supreme organ of the society and meetings of that body are required to be conducted once in a year. Co-operative Societies Act provides for convening of special general body meetings also at any time if there are specific issues to be discussed.

Chief executive of the Large-sized Adivasi Multi-purpose Co-operative Society plays a prominent and decisive role in its functioning. Like any other co-operative institution LAMPS also will have a Chief executive who acts as a link between the society and the board of directors. The Chief Executive of LAMPS was invariably used to be called 'Secretary' , but of late three LAMPS have changed the name of the designation as Manager or Managing Director. For example, name of the designation of the Chief Executive in Udupi and Kundapura LAMPS is 'Managing Director' and that in Karkala LAMPS is 'Manager'. And in the remaining 18 LAMPS, the Chief Executive is designated as 'Secretary'. Since the designation 'Secretary' is well known and most popular, we use the same in the book to mean Chief Executive of LAMPS. The role of the Chief Executive in the day-to-day functioning of the society, in its business expansion and in undertaking income-generating activities is vital. He is one person who really, by virtue of the strength of that post, has the capacity to make or mar the institution. Since tribal people are largely illiterate and have little knowledge about functioning of the society and the real benefits they can derive from it, role of the Chief Executive gets added importance. It is upto him to see that the affairs of the society are run smoothly and the benefits accrue to the members. In the actual situation in which LAMPS are placed today, where a large number of directors are ignorant of the Rules and Act guiding the management of the society, and lack knowledge about building up resources and expanding the business, the Chief Executive should necessarily play a bigger role.

Secretaries of LAMPS in Karnataka are generally of three types by virtue of the service they belong to. The first type consists of secretaries who are appointed by the society itself and who are usually called 'Paid Secretaries' to mean that they are paid by the institution itself for being in its regular service. Ten LAMPS in Karnataka State have paid secretaries. These LAMPS are Koppa, Mudigere, Mangalore, Bantwala, Belthangadi, Puttur, Sullia, Basavanahalli, Bhagamandala and Heggadadevanakote. The second type consists of secretaries who are officers belonging to the co-operation department, such as Co-operative Development Officer or Inspector of Co-operative Societies, whose services are hired by the LAMPS on a full-time basis. Only four LAMPS have such secretaries and they are Udupi, B.R. Hills, Bhatkal and Chamarajanagar LAMPS. They draw salary and allowances from the LAMPS which they would have drawn in their original department. These secretaries may serve the LAMPS for a term of three years, five years or above that and then they will be repatriated to their original service. The third type consists of secretaries who are officers belonging to co-operation department and who serve as Chief Executive-in-charge of LAMPS for a certain period. Their services will be with the Government, and they draw salary and allowances from it but serve the LAMPS only on in-charge and adhoc basis. Seven LAMPS have such secretaries and they are Hanur, Gundlupet, Hunsur, Muthathi, Thithimathi, Karkala and Kundapura.

In some LAMPS, in the beginning of their establishment Range Forest Officers also served as Secretaries-in-charge.

Since there are three types of Secretaries as far as the nature of the service is concerned, it is of significance to understand which type of the Secretary is beneficial to the society in all its angles. During interviews with the concerned people it was observed that it was a thought provoking question also. Out of fifty nine persons interviewed, who consisted of forty eight elected representatives—Presidents and Directors of LAMPS—and eleven officers—three Deputy Conservators of Forests, five Deputy Registrars of Co-operative Societies, one Block Development Officer and two Integrated Tribal Development Officers who have been closely concerned with the functioning of LAMPS, forty eight persons have been of the opinion that paid Secretary is the best person for LAMPS, seven persons were in favour of secretaries-in-charge and only four persons were for secretaries whose services are hired from the government on a full time basis. In other words, eighty one per cent of the people interviewed expressed their opinion in favour of paid secretaries, twelve per cent were in favour of secretaries-in-charge and only seven per cent were for full-time secretaries from government.

The reasons adduced in favour of their opinion are really interesting, though they are narrow in perception. Persons in favour of paid secretaries were vociferous in their argument that only this type of Chief executives can function on a full time basis and work whole heartedly for welfare of the institution by understanding the needs and problems of tribal people. The view of the supporters of Secretaries-in-charge is that as these officers draw their salary and allowances from their department, the society will be saved from the risk of bearing the burden of his salary. This, they say, will help the society to earn profits or to reduce losses. Those who are in favour of full-time Secretaries whose services are hired from the government, hold the view that since these chief executives are senior officers belonging to co-operation department, they will be an asset to serve the institution and their services can be dispensed with at any time when the society desires.

Activities of LAMPS

LAMPS is a co-operative institution and as such it can undertake any activity which is co-operative in character and which is intended to help the tribals and to solve economic problems of that section. Bye-laws of the society serve as a beacon light in all its aspects of administration and activities it can undertake. Objectives of the LAMPS are narrated in its bye-laws. A study of the objectives of all LAMPS indicates that each LAMPS has about twenty objectives which include providing short-term and medium-term credit to members, inculcating the habit of thrift and self-help among members, to undertake banking activities, to collect and sell minor forest produces, to open branches, depots and marketing centres so as to have outlets to sell commodities required by members, to provide financial assistance to members to construct residential houses, to make agreement with local authority or similar agencies for construction of road, dam, digging of well and to undertake other public works contract to provide wage employment to tribal people, so on and so forth. Hence LAMPS are expected to take all activities which can create employment opportunities, generate income and make value addition to the products they handle.

But no LAMPS in Karnataka has taken up all the activities narrated in its bye-laws. Only a few LAMPS have undertaken a large number of activities and a majority of LAMPS have restricted their activities to just two or three.

Collection and sale of minor forest produces is the major activity undertaken by LAMPS. Another important activity of LAMPS is distribution of controlled commodities, i.e., rationed goods such as rice, wheat, sugar and kerosene. Many LAMPS undertake the activity of sale of fertilisers and other agricultural inputs. Only five LAMPS have taken up banking activity on a large scale. They accept deposits of different types from members and non-members belonging to tribal community and advance loans of different types. Again, only five LAMPS have embarked upon the business of advancing short-term and medium-term loans. In other words, collection and sale of minor forest produces and distribution of controlled goods are the common activities undertaken by all LAMPS in Karnataka.

Procurement and sale of minor forest produces is a highly income generating activity. Banking activity also ensures a lucrative profit margin in that LAMPS provide a comparatively lower rate of interest on deposits and charge higher rate of interest on loans they advance. Distribution of controlled goods fetches a very low profit margin. But LAMPS find it convenient to undertake that activity as it does not require any capital investment and it is just a process of passing on the rationed goods to member and non-member card holders.

Enquiries and available data in the LAMPS have sufficiently revealed that distribution of rationed goods to card holders is also a profitable business. The idea of the author that LAMPS could very well give up this business and continue only with MFP activity and other business such as supplies of essential commodities to designated institutions was not palatable to stake holders. Their argument runs on the lines that distribution of essential articles to card holders gives an opportunity to LAMPS for interaction with members as well as non-members as also the business yields a profit margin of about five to six per cent.

At present all the LAMPS except that of Gundlupet and Muthathi have another important activity nomenclatured as "other business". This includes supplies of food grains and other articles to tribal welfare centres, hostels run by social welfare and backward classes departments. Some LAMPS have been fortunate enough to make a roaring business in this activity.

As reflected in Table 3.6, total business of all LAMPS in the State was of the order of Rs. 304.38 Lakhs in 1990-91, Rs. 1,060.40 Lakhs in 1996-97 and Rs. 834.22 Lakhs in 1998-99. Minor forest products business of these societies was to the extent of Rs. 97.92 Lakhs, Rs. 287.22 Lakhs and Rs. 217.07 Lakhs respectively in these years. They had consumer business of the value of Rs. 155.65 Lakhs, Rs. 452.67 Lakhs and Rs. 339.56 Lakhs

Table 3.6

Business Transaction of LAMPS (Rs. in Lakhs)

Sl. No.	Name of the LAMPS	1990-91			
		Minor Forest products	Consumer Business	Other Business	Total Forest
1.	LAMPS Hunsur	0.70	–	–	0.70
2.	LAMPS Heggadadevanakote	2.78	1.36	–	4.14
3.	LAMPS Chamarajanagar	8.92	2.80	–	11.72
4.	LAMPS Gundlupet	12.02	7.16	–	19.20
5.	LAMPS B.R. Hills	6.52	4.59	–	11.11
6.	LAMPS Hanur	9.34	–	–	9.34
7.	LAMPS Thithimathi	10.86	2.81	8.78	22.45
8.	LAMPS Basavanahalli	2.69	12.38	2.01	17.08
9.	LAMPS Bhagamandala	3.22	0.37	–	3.59
10.	LAMPS Koppa	1.91	43.01	–	44.92
11.	LAMPS Mudigere	–	38.00	–	38.00
12.	LAMPS Sullia	5.10	8.65	6.48	20.23
13.	LAMPS Puttur	2.07	3.54	12.16	17.77
14.	LAMPS Bantwala	–	4.21	4.40	8.61
15.	LAMPS Mangalore	–	7.52	1.22	8.74
16.	LAMPS Belthangadi	13.00	4.60	3.50	21.10
17.	LAMPS Karkala	–	–	–	–
18.	LAMPS Kundapura	4.51	2.46	0.86	7.83
19.	LAMPS Udupi	14.28	12.17	11.40	37.85
20.	LAMPS Muthathi	–	–	–	–
21.	LAMPS Bhatkal	–	–	–	–
	Total	**97.92**	**155.65**	**50.81**	**304.38**

(Table Contd...)

(Table Contd....)

Sl. No.	Name of the LAMPS	1996-97			
		Minor Forest products	Consumer Business	Other Business	Total Forest
1.	LAMPS Hunsur	1.23	5.71	–	6.94
2.	LAMPS Heggadadevanakote	8.80	2.65	0.06	11.51
3.	LAMPS Chamarajanagar	8.18	35.56	14.08	57.82
4.	LAMPS Gundlupet	2.24	2.73	–	4.97
5.	LAMPS B.R. Hills	11.32	3.16	6.00	20.48
6.	LAMPS Hanur	1.74	–	1.76	3.50
7.	LAMPS Thithimathi	4.46	10.15	6.43	21.04
8.	LAMPS Basavanahalli	5.87	51.10	6.23	63.20
9.	LAMPS Bhagamandala	27.78	0.75	0.28	28.81
10.	LAMPS Koppa	107.81	48.92	160.64	317.37
11.	LAMPS Mudigere	34.10	162.61	–	196.71
12.	LAMPS Sullia	1.87	32.60	14.15	48.62
13.	LAMPS Puttur	15.16	14.80	18.78	48.74
14.	LAMPS Bantwala	–	14.01	4.81	18.82
15.	LAMPS Mangalore	–	2.72	5.99	8.71
16.	LAMPS Belthangadi	34.58	3.97	4.68	43.23
17.	LAMPS Karkala	15.43	37.86	50.81	104.10
18.	LAMPS Kundapura	–	5.87	3.66	9.53
19.	LAMPS Udupi	6.10	17.50	22.15	45.75
20.	LAMPS Muthathi	0.55	–	–	0.55
21.	LAMPS Bhatkal	–	–	–	–
	Total	**287.22**	**452.67**	**320.51**	**217.07**

(Table Contd...)

(Table Contd....)

Sl. No.	Name of the LAMPS	1998-99			
		Minor Forest products	Consumer Business	Other Business	Total
1.	LAMPS Hunsur	2.39	3.50	0.32	6.21
2.	LAMPS Heggadadevanakote	10.98	2.00	0.24	13.22
3.	LAMPS Chamarajanagar	28.02	12.96	0.95	41.93
4.	LAMPS Gundlupet	2.35	0.90	–	3.25
5.	LAMPS B.R. Hills	8.18	3.40	5.10	16.68
6.	LAMPS Hanur	10.04	–	10.35	20.39
7.	LAMPS Thithimathi	9.52	2.10	8.40	20.02
8.	LAMPS Basavanahalli	5.00	40.48	5.23	50.71
9.	LAMPS Bhagamandala	35.85	2.03	0.48	38.36
10.	LAMPS Koppa	4.60	70.43	14.93	89.96
11.	LAMPS Mudigere	11.40	103.47	109.09	223.96
12.	LAMPS Sullia	1.87	22.23	14.06	38.16
13.	LAMPS Puttur	15.16	14.55	29.06	58.77
14.	LAMPS Bantwala	–	9.07	2.10	11.17
15.	LAMPS Mangalore	–	3.82	4.52	8.34
16.	LAMPS Belthangadi	34.58	4.03	0.66	39.27
17.	LAMPS Karkala	15.43	22.70	50.50	88.63
18.	LAMPS Kundapura	12.75	5.74	0.15	18.64
19.	LAMPS Udupi	6.10	16.15	21.45	43.70
20.	LAMPS Muthathi	2.85	–	–	2.85
21.	LAMPS Bhatkal	–	–	–	–
	Total	**217.07**	**339.56**	**277.59**	**834.23**

Source: Data personally collected from the Societies.

respectively in these years. Other business handled by these societies was of the order of Rs. 50.81 Lakhs ,Rs. 320.51 Lakhs and Rs. 279.57 Lakhs respectively in these three years.

A close look at the different types of business handled by these societies indicates that MFP business which was in a small scale in 1990-91 had gone up to substantial proportions by 1996-97 but has scaled down in 1998-99. Reduction in the forest area leased to LAMPS is the main reason for this decline. Consumer business has shown rising trend consistently. On the other hand, other business which rose considerably between 1990-91 and 1996-97 declined to a small extent in 1998-99.

Retail Business

Except for Muthathi LAMPS, all the other 19 LAMPS have opened retail outlets. These outlets serve the purpose of distribution of controlled articles to card holders and sale of non-controlled consumer goods and agricultural inputs. In some LAMPS these outlets serve as centres of collection of minor forest produces. Since each LAMPS covers in its area of operation many villages or podus, they have opened branches in the places where they can muster sufficient business.

An analysis of average monthly sales and average net profit per branch indicates that each branch, i.e., retail outlet, earns a profit of five to seven per cent on the total sales. In-depth study and enquiries have revealed that distribution of controlled articles fetches a profit margin of just four to five per cent, whereas sale of non-controlled goods and agricultural inputs provides a net profit margin of around seven to eight per cent. This amply shows that retail business, i.e., sale of controlled and non-controlled goods in all the LAMPS is profitable and there is no room to murmur that it is risky and loss-causing.

As table 3.7 indicates, altogether 19 LAMPS have total number of 72 retail outlets. These outlets are also considered as branches. Average monthly sales in these outlets vary widely from one LAMPS to the other. For example, average monthly sales at one retail outlet in Bantwala LAMPS is Rs. 90,000 whereas it is Rs. 36,000 in Hunsur LAMPS, Rs. 10,000 at Heggadadevanakote and Hanur LAMPS and less than Rs. 4,000 at B.R. Hills LAMPS.

Table 3.7

Retail Business of LAMPS

SI. No.	*Name of the LAMPS*	*No. of retail outlets*	*Average monthly sales (in Rupees)*	*Average Net Profit per month (in Rupees)*
1.	LAMPS Hunsur	2	72,000	4,000
2.	LAMPS Heggadadevanakote	2	20,000	1,200
3.	LAMPS Chamarajanagar	4	14,000	1,000
4.	LAMPS Gundlupet	2	12,000	600
5.	LAMPS B.R. Hills	4	15,000	1,000
6.	LAMPS Hanur	1	10,000	500
7.	LAMPS Thithimathi	1,	15,000	1,000
8.	LAMPS Basavanahalli	5	50,000	3,000
9.	LAMPS Bhagamandala	1	11,000	600
10.	LAMPS Koppaa	13	50,000	2,500
11.	LAMPS Mudigere	12	60,000	3,000
12.	LAMPS Sullia	10	85,000	4,500
13.	LAMPS Puttur	4	50,000	3,000
14.	LAMPS Bantwala	1	90,000	5,200
15.	LAMPS Mangalore	1	15,000	1,000
16.	LAMPS Belthangadi	2	45,000	2,600
17.	LAMPS Karkala	3	80,000	5,000
18.	LAMPS Kundapura	2	45,000	2,500
19.	LAMPS Udupi	2	52,000	3,500
20.	LAMPS Muthathi	–	–	–
21.	LAMPS Bhatkal	–	–	–

Source: Data personally collected from the societies.

Processing Activity

LAMPS are supposed to collect minor forest produces from their members and sell them at the market at a fair price so as to get a good profit margin. Many of the forest produces are in the raw form and only their processing will make them fit for use. Soapnut and honey are the most important produces which fall into this category. Processing is a very important activity in that it makes value addition to the commodity, increases marketability of the product and makes the product fit for use. Establishment of processing plant can make the LAMPS a self-reliant and profit-earning unit.

An example of lucrative business of honey processing is given here. Honey processing plant requires a capital expenditure of about Rs. 5.00 lakhs at present. LAMPS purchase honey from members at an average rate of Rs. 50 per kilogram and after processing it can be sold at Rs. 100 per kilogram. After deducting cost of labour, bottling and other services as well as depreciation of plant and machinery, each kilogram of processed honey can fetch a profit of about thirty rupees.

Soapnut processing can also provide the same advantages. Soapnut is usually purchased by LAMPS at Rs. 8 per kilogram and after processing a K.G. soapnut powder is sold at Rs. 30 in the retail market and at Rs. 23/-at the wholesale market.

LAMPS of Mudigere and Basavanahalli have set up their own soapnut processing plants. Koppa LAMPS had been getting soapnut processed at a private factory earlier, but recently it has established a plant of its own. Bhagamandala LAMPS had a honey processing unit but it has become defunct at present.

Banking Activities

Bye-laws of LAMPS provide for undertaking banking

activities. Only five LAMPS in Karnataka State have been doing banking activities. They are LAMPS of Koppa, Mudigere, Karkala, Kundapura and Udupi.

These LAMPS have introduced a number of deposit schemes and have been lending in different forms. The most usual forms in which they collect deposits from both members and non-members are pigmy schemes, savings bank scheme, fixed deposit scheme and recurring deposit scheme. LAMPS of Mudigere and Udupi have gone a step further and have introduced "LAMPS Savings Certificate" a scheme under which deposits will be accepted for a fixed term and certificates are issued to depositors in lieu of the deposited amount. These deposits bear an attractive rate of interest.

Table 3.8 indicates deposit position of these five LAMPS as on 31/03/1999.

LAMPS deploy their funds collected through different types of deposits profitably by lending in different forms. The most usual forms of lending are (i) Pigmy loans-lending upto about 75 per cent of the amount deposited by a person under pigmy scheme, (ii) Jewel loans-lending by getting the jewels pledged, (iii) salary scheme loans-lending money to salaried persons to be recovered in instalments, and (iv) loans on savings certificates.

Thus, these LAMPS have been rendering commercial banking services. Their contribution in inculcating savings and banking habit among people is immense and noteworthy.

Term Loans

Some LAMPS in Karnataka have been advancing term loans in the same way as co-operative and commercial banks do. But this activity of LAMPS should

Table 3.8

Deposits in LAMPS as on 31.3.1999 (Rs. in Lakhs)

Sl. No.	*Name of the LAMPS*	*Pigmy deposits*	*Savings bank deposits*	*Fixed deposits*	*Recurring Deposits*	*Lamps Centificates*	*Total*
1.	LAMPS Karkala	–	0.46	4.28	1.09	–	5.83
2.	LAMPS Koppa	2.20	1.22	0.75	–	–	4.17
3.	LAMPS Kundapura	0.38	0.86	0.29	–	–	1.53
4.	LAMPS Mudigere	3.66	–	5.01	–	0.16	8.83
5.	LAMPS Udupi	3.96	2.91	2.22	1.04	0.20	10.33

Source: Data personally collected from the societies.

not be construed to mean their role of acting as conduit to dole out funds sanctioned by government in different schemes, or giving loans to members out of borrowed funds from the district central co-operative banks. Almost all the LAMPS in the State have performed this activity in one or two years and had a very bitter experience before many of them gave it up. LAMPS used to advance medium term loans to members usually to purchase bullock and cart or under integrated rural development programme by borrowing funds from district central co-operative banks. Subsidy portion was given by the government and LAMPS used their own funds to meet the loan portion. Enquiries have revealed that about 80 per cent of these loans advanced by LAMPS were misutilised and were never repaid. Only a few LAMPS which had an assured recovery of a good percentage are advancing these loans at present.

But, of late, some LAMPS have been advancing short-term loans also called crop loans and medium term loans for a number of purposes. These purposes mainly include raising of crop, digging well, installation of pumpset, coffee plantation, sericulture, purchase of vehicles and so on.

Only five LAMPS have so far undertaken this activity on a big scale. They are LAMPS of Koppa, Mudigere, Udupi, Karkala and Kundapura. They have advanced these loans for paddy, coffee and cardamom crops, poultry, digging of wells and purchase of pumpsets. Total number of persons availing short term and medium term loans and total amount of these loans lent by these five LAMPS as on 31.3.1999 has been indicated in Table 3.9.

Minor Forest Produces Business

As has been pointed out else where, collection and sale of minor forest produces is the major activity of LAMPS and it is a highly income generating activity. Bawa

Table 3.9

Advances of Term Loans by LAMPS (as on 31.3.1999)

Sl. No.	*Name of the Lamps*	*S.T. Loan*		*M.T. Loan*	
		Persons	*Amount*	*Persons*	*Amount*
1.	LAMPS Karkala	09	0.74	24	3.72
2.	LAMPS Koppa	04	0.16	10	2.64
3.	LAMPS Mudigere	98	10.96	35	3.70
4.	LAMPS Udupi	40	3.32	67	6.87
5.	LAMPS Kundapura	–	–	13	1.69
	Total	**151**	**15.18**	**149**	**18.62**

Source: Data personally collected from the societies.

Committee had visualized that LAMPS should develop as centres of tribal evolution. This was seen to be achieved on the one hand by giving a fair remuneration to the tribals for the minor forest produces they collect, and on the other hand by catering to the needs of the tribals so as to bring about economic and social transformation in the tribal community. Since LAMPS are institutions the members of which are tribal people living in forest and hill areas and eking out their livelihood mainly by collecting and selling forest based resources, it is natural that major activity of LAMPS is expected to be procurement and sale of minor forest produces. Since forests and their products belong to the Government which is represented by Karnataka Forest Department, tribal people have only usufructuary right over these produces. In other words, tribal people can only extract and sell these produces but cannot claim right of possession over forests and their resources. LAMPS are required to get the forest area on lease by paying royalty to the Karnataka Forest Department. Each LAMPS submits a proposal with application to the Karnataka State Forest Department for grant of a lease to collect minor forest produces in its area of operation. The Forest Department grants the lease for some designated areas. The lease period will be usually for two years, after the expiry of which the LAMPS has to submit a fresh proposal for grant of lease.

The LAMPS announces the price to be paid to the tribal collector for each product before its season begins. Tribals collect the produces and deliver it to the LAMPS. The society collects the produces either at its headquarters, or at its branches or in other designated places. Branches in most of the LAMPS are serving as centres of MFP collection. Payment for the produce is made to the tribals soon after it is delivered or after a gap of two or three days. A majority of the LAMPS have practice of making advance payment to the tribal collectors and getting it settled while making payment to the produce when it is delivered. As shown in Table 3.10, altogether 20 LAMPS have a total forest area of 20,54,484 acres in their jurisdiction. Out of this area 4,49,527 acres i.e., 22 per cent of the area is leased out to LAMPS to collect minor forest produces. In fact, no forest area is leased out to Udupi and Kundapura LAMPS. They have been permitted to collect dhoopa from road side trees in the area of their operation on payment of royalty to the forest department.

Karnataka State Forest Department has a list of 43 minor forest products which the LAMPS are allowed to collect. But a look at the minor forest products business of LAMPS shows that procurement and sale is restricted to just about ten to fifteen items. Important minor forest products collected by LAMPS in the state are Honey, Soapnut, Amla also called Nellikai, Wax, Lac, Dhoopa (Tree bark), Tree mass, Antuwala (Sapindus emarginatus), and some leaves and roots which are of medicinal value. Observations have revealed that tree mass is collected only to the extent of about 10 per cent of the availability. Thus, there are possibilities for its further extraction.

It is not to be understood that everything is smooth for LAMPS as far as minor forest produces business is concerned. Grievances of LAMPS in this regard are many. The problems they encounter, to put in their own version, are noncooperation from the state Forest Department, undue delay in granting lease for the forest area, arbitrary fixation of the lease amount, leasing out only a part of the forest area, collecting royalty even for the forests which do not bear any produce so on and so forth. The representatives of LAMPS have complained about these in many meetings and even individually to the State Forest Department and also to the Karnataka State Government. There have been threadbare discussions in a number of meetings which have been represented by the officers of

Table 3.10

Access to Forests

SI. NO.	*Name of the LAMPS*	*Forest Area in LAMPS jurisdiction (Acres)*	*Area Leased to LAMPS (Acres)*	*Percentage of area allotted to LAMPS to total forest area*
1.	LAMPS Hunsur	19,231	2,200	11
2.	LAMPS Heggadadevanakote	81,587	15,470	19
3.	LAMPS Chamarajanagar	66,450	60,590	91
4.	LAMPS Gundlupet	1,10,802	20,762	19
5.	LAMPS B.R. Hills	26,155	24,000	92
6.	LAMPS Hanur	4,77,350	15,318	03
7.	LAMPS Thithimathi	1,63,598	66,690	41
8.	LAMPS Basavanahalli	51,497	7,286	14
9.	LAMPS Bhagamandala	1,17,360	4,593	04
10.	LAMPS Koppa	1,17,952	23,919	20

(Table Contd...)

(Table Contd....)

Sl. NO.	*Name of the LAMPS*	*Forest Area in LAMPS jurisdiction (Acres)*	*Area Leased to LAMPS (Acres)*	*Percentage of area allotted to LAMPS to total forest area*
11.	LAMPS Mudigere	75,592	19,000	25
12.	LAMPS Sullia	1,06,907	1,06,000	99
13.	LAMPS Puttur	67,609	16,500	24
14.	LAMPS Bantwala	73,400	12,520	17
15.	LAMPS Mangalore	–	–	–
16.	LAMPS Belthangadi	1,22,848	20,145	16
17.	LAMPS Karkala	84,062	11,920	14
18.	LAMPS Kundapura	1,54,634	9,300	06
19.	LAMPS Udupi	1,18,000	11,574	10
20.	LAMPS Muthathi	19,450	1,740	09
21.	LAMPS Bhatkal	NA	NA	NA
	Total	**20,54,484**	**4,49,527**	-

Source: Data personally collected from the Societies.

the State Forest Department, as also Co-operation Department and representatives of LAMPS. But nothing has come out so far except reduction of royalty to a token amount of Rs. 100 and grievances of the LAMPS continue.

Some of the important lacunae noticed in granting access to forest areas and forest produces are as follows.

1. Inspite of a directive of the State Government that MFP leases have to be granted to LAMPS wherever they exist, Karnataka Forest Department has excluded many LAMPS from access to forest areas. For example, Hanur LAMPS was always excluded from access to 3 out of 5 ranges, Mudigere LAMPS was always excluded from access to one out of four ranges, Bantwala LAMPS has been allotted forest areas of five villages belonging to a range of the neighbouring taluka. It has been excluded from access to forest areas of Bantwala taluka, i.e. the actual area of its operation!

In such cases private collectors are preferred to LAMPS and they get the leases in auction. In other words, writ of the State Forest Department runs as it determines in which forest areas the access has to be granted.

2. Though LAMPS are to be solely given right to harvest minor forest produces in the areas where they exist, the State Forest Department has sometimes granted collection rights over some products to private contracts. An important case that can be cited in this regard is that of deer antlers where only private contractors are granted rights to collect this resource even now. Collection and sale of deer antlers is a highly profitable business and LAMPS are deprived of this.

3. Karnataka Forest Department determines the amount of royalty to be paid by the LAMPS for the lease. But the lease amounts are arbitrarily fixed

and arbitrarily hiked. In the last 15 years lease amount has been arbitrarily hiked by about 600 percent. There are no proper guidelines to determine the lease amount and hence local forest officials are vested with enormous discretionary powers. Instances are not lacking where forest officials have helped the tribals by using this discretionary power. But by and large, the forest department's intention has been to maximise its revenues and this could be done at the cost of LAMPS.

The Government of Karnataka passed a number of orders in 1976,1977,1982, 1987 and 2001 giving concessions to LAMPS on the lease amounts. These concessions were in the form of rebate ranging from 17.5 per cent to 35 per cent in different years. But the scheme of providing rebate on the lease amounts is not in vogue since the year 1990. This scheme, when it was in operation, was of some help to the LAMPS. The Karnataka Government's order of 2001 has reduced the lease amount from 1st June 2001 to a nominal sum of Rs. 100 per year for all the items involved in the lease.

4. LAMPS is expected to apply to the forest department in the month of July of a certain year to obtain lease for the ensuing two year period. But there have been instances of undue delay on the part of the forest department in granting lease. Sometimes this delay has been to the extent of seven to eight months and during this period LAMPS are prevented from extracting minor forest produces. Lease will be granted with retrospective effect, and lease amount will be collected in full for the entire period. But owing to undue delay in granting lease, by the time LAMPS are permitted to harvest minor forest produces, a significant portion of the produce will be lost. As a result, LAMPS are forced to bear the loss of revenue.

5. Rules of the Karnataka Forest Department require issuance of permits for entry of tribals and vehicles into forests and for transport of MFP. Even after lease is granted, harassment by field level staff of the forest department continues. Sometimes issuance of permits is delayed and entry of tribals into forests is restricted. Citing the fear of forest fires, the forest department often suspends MFP collection in the months of March and April.

This is the season for collection of many important forest produces like soapnut, tamarind, antuwala and gum. As a result, harvesting by the LAMPS will be reduced and they suffer losses.

6. In recent years more forest areas are converted into national parks and wild life sanctuaries. Hence, forest areas allocated have depleted drastically over the years and a number of LAMPS in the state have suffered from this depletion. This is one of the main reasons for reduced variety of minor forest produces and declining share of MFP revenues in total revenues of LAMPS.
7. According to the wild life Act of 1982, minor forest produces cannot be collected from protected areas such as wildlife sanctuaries and national parks. Hence LAMPS cannot have access to these areas to harvest MFP. But clandestine collection of MFP by private contractors with the connivance of forest officials is rampant.
8. Although LAMPS have exclusive rights to collect MFP from the designated area, this right cannot always be enforced on behalf of tribal collectors. They have still to depend upon forest officials for enforcement of right to collect. Non-tribals and private contractors take this advantage and

indulge in collection of MFP even in designated areas. As a result, a huge portion of MFP is lost and LAMPS are the sufferers.

Table 3.11

Accumulated Profit or Loss of LAMPS (as on 31.3.1999)

(Rs. in Lakhs)

Sl. No.	Name of the LAMPS	Accumulated Profit	Accumulated Loss
1.	LAMPS Hunsur	–	8.48
2.	LAMPS Heggadadevanakote	–	2.19
3.	LAMPS Chamarajanagar	23.92	–
4.	LAMPS Gundlupet	–	7.20
5.	LAMPS B.R. Hills	0.10	–
6.	LAMPS Hanur	–	0.43
7.	LAMPS Thithimathi	–	6.00
8.	LAMPS Basavanahalli	1.59	–
9.	LAMPS Bhagamandala	1.66	–
10.	LAMPS Koppa	0.26	–
11.	LAMPS Mudigere	0.44	–
12.	LAMPS Sullia	4.26	–
13.	LAMPS Puttur	5.99	–
14.	LAMPS Bantwala	–	4.32
15.	LAMPS Mangalore	–	4.68
16.	LAMPS Belthangadi	–	11.25
17.	LAMPS Karkala	–	10.52
18.	LAMPS Kundapura	0.02	–
19.	LAMPS Udupi	0.35	–
20.	LAMPS Muthathi	3.45	–
21.	LAMPS Bhatkal	0.82	–
	Total	**42.86**	**55.07**

Source: Data personally collected from the societies.

Table 3.11 clearly brings out that out of twenty one LAMPS in the state 12 LAMPS had earned accumulated profit of a total amount of Rs. 42.86 Lakhs as at the end of the financial year 1999. On the other hand nine LAMPS had incurred accumulated losses which totally amounted to Rs. 55.07 lakhs.

Only two LAMPS, Chamarajanagar with an accumulated profit amount of Rs. 23.92 lakhs and Puttur with an accumulated profit amount of Rs. 5.99 Lakhs, fall into the category of having had an accumulated profit of above Rs. 5.00 Lakhs. Accumulated profit amount of Sullia LAMPS with Rs. 4.26 Lakhs is also remarkable. In other LAMPS accumulated profit was to the tune of just above Rs. 1.00 Lakhs amount each or a paltry sum of a few thousands of rupees. Accumulated profit amount of Kundapura LAMPS had been of the order of a meagre two thousand rupees.

Except for Hanur LAMPS, each of the other eight LAMPS had a huge amount of accumulated losses. The amount of accumulated losses crossed Rs. 10 Lakhs in the case of Karkala and Belthangadi LAMPS. Altogether, nine LAMPS had a total accumulated loss to the tune of Rs. 55.07 Lakhs as at the end of the financial year 1999.

Economic and Social Status of Members

An analysis of economic and social status of tribal members will give an insight into their life style, living conditions, the rate of literacy among them etc., This will help us to understand the tribal economy and whether the tribals have remained far away from the mainstream or whether there are features of assimilation with the other part of the society.

Economic and social status was one of the important factors ascertained during the visits paid to LAMPS and tribal villages, by interviewing the concerned persons.

Out of 136 tribal members, covering 12 LAMPS, who were interviewed exhibited almost similar life styles and social conditions but differed a little as far their economic conditions are concerned.

Table 3.12

Economic Status of Members

	Number of Members Interviewed		136
I.	Ownership of land		
	(i)	Number of persons owning land	55
	(ii)	Number of landless persons	81
	Percentage of landholders to total members		
II.	Size of holding		
	(i)	Upto 2 acres	49
	(ii)	2 to 5 acres	06
	(iii)	Above 5 acres	
III.	Cropping pattern		
	(i)	Number of persons growing commercial crops	13
	(ii)	Number of persons growing traditional crops	42
	(iii)	Percentage of persons growing commercial crops	24
	(iv)	Percentage of persons growing traditional crops	76
IV.	Irrigation		
	(i)	Number of persons having irrigation facilities	27
	(ii)	Extent of land irrigated (acres)	58
	(iii)	Number of persons having dry land	28
	(iv)	Extent of Dry land (acres)	68
V.	Method of irrigation		
	(i)	Well	17
	(ii)	Pond	06
	(iii)	Other Sources	04
VI.	Value of other Assets, Vessels, Furniture, Television, Radio, Vehicle, etc.,		
	(i)	Upto Rs. 1,000	46
	(ii)	Rs. 2,001 to 4,000	58
	(iii)	Rs. 4,001 and above	32

(Table Contd...)

(Table Contd....)

VII.	Annual Income (No. of persons)		
	(i)	Upto Rs. 4,000/-	26
	(ii)	Rs. 4,001 to Rs. 8,000	66
	(iii)	Rs. 8,001 to Rs. 12,000	32
	(iv)	Rs. 12,001 and above	12
VIII.	Housing facilities		
	(i)	Number of persons having tiled roofing houses	65
	(ii)	Number of persons having sheds	71
IX.	*(i)*	Number of persons owning livestock	12
	(ii)	Percentage of persons owning livestock	09

Source: Data personally collected from the societies.

Table 3.12 indicates that out of 136 tribal members 55 persons own land. The percentage of landholders is 43. Landless persons among tribal members far outstrip the number and percentage of land holders.

Landholdings of tribal members are usually of two types-

(i) Own land sanctioned by the government and (ii) forest land which is cultivated by tribal members for some years and to be considered as their own, but over which they do not have possession certificates. Out of 55 tribal members, 32 persons have own land sanctioned by the government and the remaining 23 own land doled out by the forest department.

Size of holdings gives a true picture of the agrarian economy of the tribal society. Forty nine persons own land less than 2 acres each and only six persons have the ownership between 2 and 5 acres each. The percentage of land holders below 2 acres is 89 and of those owning between 2 and 5 acres is 11. No tribal member out of 136 persons owned above 5 acres of land. In other words, an overwhelming number of members of LAMPS belongs to the category of very small holders. In some areas many tribals have been given 2 acres of land by the forest department in recent years and this has converted them as landholders at least for namesake.

Of the 55 agriculturist members, 42 are still doing subsistence agriculture by growing paddy, ragi and such other traditional crops. On the other hand 13 persons have been growing commercial crops such as coffee and cotton. Many a tribal member in Chikmagalur and Coorg districts and also in the area of LAMPS of B.R. Hills and Chamarajanagar own coffee plantations though of very small acreage.

Irrigation facility is another important factor which plays a decisive role in determining economic conditions of agriculturists. Twenty seven tribal members had irrigation facilities to their land whereas the remaining 28 members were devoid of irrigation facilities to their land and which was categorised as dry. That means to say on a rough estimate 50 per cent of the land holders had irrigation facilities and the remaining 50 per cent landholdings were dry.

Seventeen persons had wells as sources of irrigation, six persons had ponds and small tanks for irrigation facilities and four persons had other sources such as rivulets and gorges. In other words the extent of natural irrigation and artificial irrigation in the tribal agriculture is of the order of 15 per cent and 85 per cent respectively.

Out of 17 wells, nine wells were dug under Million wells scheme, a programme of the Government of India under which irrigation wells are dug free of cost in the lands of scheduled castes and scheduled tribes people. Out of the remaining eight wells, six were dug by the members by obtaining loan from the LAMPS in which they are members and two were dug by obtaining loan from commercial banks. Fourteen persons had diesel pumpsets and three persons had electric pumpsets to lift water from wells.

A view into the value of other assets such as vessels, furniture, radio, vehicle, television, etc., possessed by tribal members provides rather a pathetic picture. Of total number of 136 members, 46 persons owned other assets worth less than Rs. 1,000 each. Their other assets included mainly some vessels. Fifty eight persons each had assets worth above Rs. 1,000 and less than Rs. 4,000. Only 32 members each possessed other assets worth above Rs. 4,000. Only 16 persons possessed radios and only two persons owned television.

Of the 55 agriculturists, 42 persons used improved seeds, pesticides and chemical fertilisers. The remaining 13 persons did not possess any interest to use improved methods of agriculture.

Majority of tribal members interviewed, i.e., 66 of the 136, had an annual income ranging between Rs. 4,001 and Rs. 8,000. Only 12 persons had annual income above Rs. 12,000.

Housing facilities had by the members are yet another indicator of their economic status. Sixty five persons own houses having tiled roofings whereas 71 members have sheds of grass which are badly equipped and inconvenient for living. Of the 65 houses of tiled roofings, 63 are the houses granted by the beneficiary oriented governmental schemes of Ashraya, Indira Avas Yojana etc. Only two houses were built by the tribal members on their own. This amply explains the extent to which the tribal society is dependent upon government assistance and the way in which it is under the mercy of the government. This also voluminously speaks of poverty existing in the tribal economy. Almost all the houses have just two portions and hence are not properly accommodative.

Only 12 tribal members out of the 136 interviewed owned livestock. Again, each of the 12 members owns just one or two cattle, their livestock property is not much of a worth and it has failed to make any dent in bringing about an improvement in the tribal economy.

Of the 136 members across 12 LAMPS, 52 persons were literate, i.e., they knew elementary reading and writing. In other words, literacy among tribal members is to the extent of 38 per cent which is far below the state average. The percentage of literacy in Karnataka state was 56 per cent according to 1991 census. But the rate of literacy among tribal members has a very large variation from one LAMPS to the other. Taken on an average for all the members, rate of literacy among the members of Koppa LAMPS is around 80 per cent, among members of Udupi LAMPS it is about 48 per cent, among members of Thithimathi LAMPS it is about 20 per cent and among members of Heggadadevanakote LAMPS it is about just 12 per cent.

Table 3.13

Social Status of Members

I.	Literacy	
	(i) Number of literate members	52
	(ii) Percentage of literacy	38
II.	Visits to LAMPS	
	(i) Number of members visiting LAMPS frequently	109
	(ii) Percentage to the total	80
	(iii) Number of members visiting LAMPS occasionally	27
	(iv) Percentage to the total	20
III.	Attendance in the General Body Meetings	
	(i) Average number of members attending General Body Meetings	98
	(ii) Percentage to the total	72

(Table Contd...)

(Table Contd....)

IV.	Contacts with officials	
	(i) Number of members having official contacts	06
	(ii) Percentage to the total	04
V.	Migration	
	(i) Number of members migrated from other places	21
	(ii) Percentage to the total	15
	(iii) Number of members residing in the place from time immemorial	115
VI.	Membership in other co-operatives	
	(i) Number of persons with Membership in other co-operative societies	44
	(ii) Percentage to the total	32

Source: Data personally collected from the societies.

Visits of members to LAMPS is another important factor with the help of which members' participation can be assessed. An overwhelming number of tribal members used to visit the society very frequently, i.e., once in a week or twice in a week. Of the 136 sample tribals, 109 visited the LAMPS frequently and only 27 visited occasionally, i.e., once in a month or in two months. The percentages of frequent visitors and occasional visitors work out to be 80.15 and 19.85 respectively. Members are used to visit the LAMPS to obtain loans, to sell produces, to get sales proceeds, to repay loans etc., Frequency of their visits indicates their association with the working of the society.

Attendance in general body meetings is appreciably good. Thirty eight persons among the sample tribals attended the general body meetings in LAMPS which works out to be 28 percent. In otherwords, 72 per cent of the sample tribals did not attend these meetings.

Tribal members fare very badly as far as their contact with the officials is concerned. They could come in contact with many officials like Gram Sevaks, Tahsildars, Block Development officers, Tribal Development Officers,

Assistant Registrar of Co-operative Societies etc., to ameliorate their problems or in the course of normal functioning of the society. Of the 136 sample tribals, only 6 persons had contacts with local and taluka level officials. In other words only about 4.4 per cent of the sample tribals had contacts with officials. Contacts of only a handful of members as has been indicated is mainly with the Co-operative Development officer, Inspector of Co-operative Societies and Tribal Development Officer.

Contacts of tribal members with non-officials was also surveyed. About 92 per cent of the members had no contacts with any non-officials. Only eight per cent had contacts with village level leader, usually Gram Panchayat member and LAMPS President.

Tribal system is usually characterised by migration. Tribals shift from place to place in search of employment, for hunting and in pursuit of agricultural vocation. 115 of the sample tribals, i.e., 85 per cent of the tribal members have been residing in their places from time immemorial. Only 21 of the sample tribals, i.e., 15 per cent of the tribal members migrated from other places one or two generations ago. What was found in the study was Marathi Naiks, a tribe most popularly found in South Canara, Udupi and parts of Chickmagalur districts have migrated from Maharashtra about 60 to 70 years ago. The opinion arrived at from this analysis is that the tribes, with the exception of a few like Hakki Pikki who are really nomadic and who change the place frequently for hunting and food gathering, are following a settled life and settled agriculture.

Other types of co-operative societies such as, credit, consumers and marketing are also functioning in the area of operation of LAMPS. Since LAMPS can provide all types of assistance to their members, i.e., tribal people, it is of interest to understand whether members of LAMPS have enrolled themselves as members in other co-operative societies. It was gathered that 44 of the sample tribals, i.e., 32 per cent of the 136 tribal members had membership in other societies particularly in credit societies in the area of operation of LAMPS. It was found that they have taken membership particularly in credit societies in order to obtain loans for seasonal agricultural operations.

Status of Members of the Committee of Management

Board of directors, also called committee of management is an important organ in the governance of the society which has far reaching powers. Members of the committee are elected by the members of the society once in five years as per Provisions of Co-operative Societies amended Act of 1997. Elected members of the committee represent the members in the administration of the society and they have a wider say in its management. This highlights the fact that the elected members or directors should be more vigilant, knowledgeable and be able to take progressive decisions in the interest of the institution.

Table 3.14

Economic Status of the Members of the Committee of Management

		Number of Members	*Percentage to the total*
	Sample Members 48		
1.	Annual Income		
(i)	Upto Rs. 10,000	15	31
(ii)	Rs. 10,001 to Rs. 20,000	18	38
(iii)	Rs. 20,001 to Rs. 30,000	13	27
(iv)	Rs. 30,001 to above	02	04
2.	Ownership of land		
(i)	Number of Members owning land	41	85
(ii)	Landless persons	07	15

(Table Contd...)

(Table Contd....)

3.	Size of land holding		
(i)	Upto 2 acres	09	22
(ii)	2 acres to 5 acres	16	39
(iii)	5 acres to 10 acres	14	34
(iv)	10 acres and above	02	05
4.	Irrigation		
(i)	Irrigated land	33	80
(ii)	Dry land	08	20
5.	Mode of Irrigation		
(i)	Well	19	58
(ii)	Pond	04	12
(iii)	Other sources	10	30
6.	Value of other properties (Furniture, Television, Radio, vehicles etc.,)		
(i)	Upto Rs. 5,000	08	17
(ii)	Rs. 5,001 to Rs. 10,000	17	35
(iii)	Rs. 10,001 to Rs. 20,000	14	29
(iv)	Rs. 20,001 and above	09	19

Source: Data personally collected from the societies.

In this background, an analysis of economic and social status of elected members of the committee of management, their knowledge of the Act and Rules and their capacity to take decisions serves as an important guide to understand the importance of the governing body.

Of the 48 sample members of the committee of management, 32 per cent had the annual income below Rs. 10,000. The percentage of members of the committee who had annual income between Rs. 10,001 and Rs. 20,000 was 38, between Rs. 20,001 and 30,000 was 27 and between Rs. 30,001 and above was just four.

Of the sample tribals 85 per cent owned land and 15 per cent are landless people.

Of the 41 land holders, 22 per cent owned below 2 acres each; 39 per cent owned between 2 and 5 acres each,

34 per cent owned between 5 and 10 acres and just 5 per cent owned more than 10 acres each. Eighty per cent of the land holder members had irrigation facilities to their land where as 20 per cent of the land holders had no irrigation facilities.

A look at the value of other properties owned by members of the committee helps us to assess their economic status in a more appropriate way. Of the 48 sample tribals, 17 per cent possessed other properties valued less than Rs. 5,000, 35 per cent had other properties the value of which was between Rs. 5,001 and Rs. 10,000, the value of other properties of each of the 29 per cent members was between Rs. 10,001 and Rs. 20,000. Only 19 per cent of the sample tribals possessed assets more than Rs. 20,000 each.

Table 3.15

Social Status of Members of the Committee of Management

	Number of Members	*Percentage to the total*
1. Literacy		
(i) Literates	41	85
(ii) Illiterates	07	15
2. Educational Level of Literate Members		
(i) Upto 4th Standard	20	49
(ii) 5th Standard to 8th Standard	12	29
(iii) 8th Standard to Pre-University course	08	20
(iv) Graduates	01	02
3. Understanding of the Act and Rules		
(i) Those who have understood the implications of Act and Rules	13	27
(ii) Those who have not understood	35	73
4. Participation in Management		
(i) Attendance in the Board meetings	41	85
(ii) Attendance in the General Body Meetings	43	89

Source: Data personally collected from the Societies.

Table 3.15 indicates that of 48 sample tribals the percentage of literates and illiterates is 85 and 15 respectively. Forty nine per cent of the literate members have education level upto 4th standard, 29 per cent have education level between 5th and 8th standard and 20 per cent have education level between 8th standard and pre-university course. Only one person is graduate.

Another interesting piece of information is that 73 per cent of the sample tribals did not have a knowledge of the Co-operative Societies Act and the Rules. Only 27 per cent understood their implications.

Attendance of members of the committee at board meetings and general body meetings has been unusually good. Attendance of directors in an average of five meetings in each of the 12 LAMPS was taken to arrive at a conclusion. This has revealed that of the 48 sample directors, 41 attended board meetings regularly. A study of the latest general body meeting in 12 LAMPS has brought out the fact that 43 of the 48 sample directors attended these meetings which means the attendance was 89 per cent.

Employment of Tribals in LAMPS

It is of utmost significance to unravel whether the LAMPS have contributed to bring about tribal welfare and to empower the tribals or not. One important criterion in this regard has been employment opportunities provided by LAMPS in their officialdom. Since LAMPS are tribal societies, it is pertinent if a large section of their employees is from tribal community only. This will definitely go a long way in tribal welfare and tribal empowerment.

The following table indicates total number of employees in each of the 20 LAMPS in Karnataka and the number of tribal employees among them.

Table 3.16

Tribal Employment in LAMPS

Sl. No.	*Name of the LAMPS*	*Total number of lower level employees*	*Number of tribals among total employees*
1.	LAMPS Hunsur	07	Nil
2.	LAMPS Heggadadevanakote	05	03
3.	LAMPS Chamarajanagar	08	03
4.	LAMPS Gundlupet	01	01
5.	LAMPS B.R. Hills	09	04
6.	LAMPS Hanur	06	Nil
7.	LAMPS Thithimathi	05	03
8.	LAMPS Basavananalli	06	02
9.	LAMPS Bhagamandala	03	02
10	LAMPS Koppa	12	03
11.	LAMPS Mudigere	09	01
12.	LAMPS Sullia	09	05
13.	LAMPS Puttur	08	07
14.	LAMPS Bantwala	05	02
15.	LAMPS Mangalore	01	01
16.	LAMPS Belthangadi	02	Nil
17.	LAMPS Karkala	11	07
18.	LAMPS Kundapura	05	03
19.	LAMPS Udupi	04	01
20.	LAMPS Muthathi	01	01
21.	LAMPS Bhatkal	03	03
	Total	**120**	**52**

Source: Data personally collected from the societies.

Table 3.16 reveals that in all the 21 LAMPS put together, there are 120 lower level employees, i.e., employees other than the secretary. Of the 120 total number of employees 52 belonged to tribal community. LAMPS of Hunsur, Hanur and Belthangadi have no tribal employees in them. Maximum number of tribal employees is in LAMPS Puttur, and Bhatkal. In the former, of 8 lower level employees 7 belong to tribal category and in the latter, all the three belong to the tribal category. The percentage of tribal employees among total number of lower level employees of all the LAMPS is 44.

Meetings of Board and General Body

One of the important principles of Co-operation is democratic control. LAMPS, being Co-operative institutions, are expected to function in a democratic manner. Relevant rules and bye-laws of these institutions insist that they have to arrange meeting of the committee of management at least once in a month. But there is no bar to call any number of meetings in a month if there are very important and emergent issues to be discussed.

It is not unusual to find that many institutions do not arrange board meetings for months together on the plea that there are no subjects to be discussed or for the simple reason that they hesitate to function in a democratic way. Karnataka Co-operative Societies Act and bye-laws of co-operative institutions ordain that general body meetings have to be held every year and before 30th September of that particular year. But instances were not uncommon where some institutions had not held general body meetings for decades together.

In this background, an attempt is made to get a view of the number of board meetings held in the LAMPS in the latest year, i.e., 1998-99 and the latest general body meeting held.

Table 3.17 indicates that all the 21 LAMPS in Karnataka have conducted their latest general body meetings in the year 1999, the implication of which is that they have complied with the Act and the Rules.

Table 3.17

Meetings in LAMPS

Sl. No.	*Name of the LAMPS*	*Number of Board meetings held in 1998-99*	*Year of Latest General Body Meeting held*
1.	LAMPS Hunsur	08	1999
2.	LAMPS Heggadadevanakote	05	1999
3.	LAMPS Chamarajanagar	12	1999
4.	LAMPS Gundlupet	05	1999
5.	LAMPS B.R. Hills	09	1999
6.	LAMPS Hanur	11	1999
7.	LAMPS Thithimathi	11	1999
8.	LAMPS Basavanahalli	12	1999
9.	LAMPS Bhagamandala	08	1999
10.	LAMPS Koppa	10	1999
11.	LAMPS Mudigere	12	1999
12.	LAMPS Sullia	12	1999
13.	LAMPS Puttur	10	1999
14.	LAMPS Bantwala	12	1999
15.	LAMPS Mangalore	08	1999
16.	LAMPS Belthangasdi	10	1999
17.	LAMPS Karkala	12	1999
18.	LAMPS Kundapura	16	1999
19	LAMPS Udupi	13	1999
20.	LAMPS Muthathi	06	1999
21.	LAMPS Bhatkal	NA	1999

Source: Data personally collected from the societies.

It has been found that 12 LAMPS did not conduct board meetings every month as is envisaged in the Act and the Rules. Only 8 LAMPS have conducted these meetings every month. LAMPS of B.R. Hills and Udupi have held a few emergent meetings apart from regular board meetings.

Payment of Dividend on Shares

One of the prominent sources of funds to co-operative institutions is share capital contributed by their members. Many institutions have been fortunate enough to get a huge amount of share capital also from government. It is the duty of the society to declare and pay dividend on the shares of members and the government out of its net profit. Only when the dividend is paid to members they feel their involvement and participation in the activities of the society.

It is of interest to know that except for four LAMPS of Udupi, kundapura, Puttur and Karkala no LAMPS has paid dividend on share capital. Udupi, Karkala and Kundapura LAMPS have declared dividend of one per cent out of their total net profits and have transferred it to members' welfare fund. They have not actually paid dividend to members. It was found that only Puttur LAMPS had made payment of money to members in lieu of dividend.

This is really a bad tale. Even LAMPS which have a huge amount of accumulated profits as well as those which have earned operative profits in certain years have not bothered to pay dividend on shares of members and of the government. Hence majority of LAMPS have failed to honour the principle of co-operative business of payment of dividend on the shares. This seems to be one predominant reason for failure of LAMPS in invoking involvement and participation of members in their activities on a large scale.

Performance of LAMPS in Karnataka

Whether the LAMPS have been a success in bringing about welfare of tribals and in the socio-economic transformation of the tribal system has to be judged by their performance over the years. LAMPS have been primarily undertaking the activity of collection and sale of minor forest produces. But all the LAMPS in Karnataka have been able to take up some more activities and to diversify their business. Performance of LAMPS has to be assessed in terms of their success in procurement and marketing of MFP, service of members and attainment of sustainable viability. Hence their performance is evaluated from three different perspectives: economic, social and ecological. To be successful in their operation, LAMPS should mobilise economic gains and be able to develop managerial capacity among the tribals. Again, if the economic gains are to be sustained, it should be seen that the resources from which they are derived are not depleted.

Economic performance of LAMPS has to be evaluated in terms of their financial viability, both short-term and long-term, their capacity in earning revenues and in bringing about a change in the economic conditions of the members.

Social performance is assessed in terms of ability of the LAMPS to enrol potential members, their ability in developing participatory and managerial skills among the tribals and their ability in bringing about equity in the distribution of gains.

Ecological performance of LAMPS pertains mainly to their MFP activity. Sustainability needs to be ensured in the collection of produces and in the growth of species. If the LAMPS should be able to collect more and more produce and sustain its business, the average physical availability of each product should remain non-diminishing over generations and MFP extraction activities should not have negative impacts on the ecosystem and on other species in the forests.

Economic Performance

Economic performance of LAMPS in Karnataka is mixed. Justification for this can be found in their profitability, viability, earnings of revenues and the services they have been providing to the members.

In terms of short-term viability, though the performance appears to be mixed, it has seen an improvement over the years. The number of LAMPS which had incurred operating losses were 13 out of 19 in 1992-93, 6 out 19 in 1994-95, and 5 out of 20 in 1998-99. Hence, the percentage of societies to the total which had incurred losses for the operating year has come down from 68.42 in 1992-93 to 25.00 in 1998-99. Sustainable viability or long-term performance of LAMPS also provides a mixed picture. The number of societies which had a net accumulated loss was 12 in 1992-93, 15 in 1994-95 and 9 in 1998-99. The percentage of societies to the total which had a net accumulated loss had come down from 63.16 in 1992-93 to 45.00 in 1998-99.

In terms of earnings of revenue, the performance of LAMPS in karnataka is good so far. Their earnings from business can be broadly classified into three categories, namely MFP activities, consumer business and loaning. The first activity is done by a very few and the last activity is undertaken by only a few societies. But the second activity is undertaken by all the LAMPS. A study into the working results of these activities has revealed that all these yield good profit margins though in different proportions. But the earnings of LAMPS in MFP activities is higher than their earnings in non-MFP activities. It is to be added that enquiries have revealed and analyses of working of these societies have shown that no business handled by LAMPS is loss causing. Only because of misuse of funds in some LAMPS, faulty policy on the part of the government, lack of repayment of loans advanced by these societies and absence of good price for the product they sell, are some of the important reasons why some LAMPS have not been faring so well as expected.

The main point to be debated is whether the organisation of LAMPS has economically benefited the MFP collectors. This question yields a positive answer. LAMPS have been able to provide better prices to the collectors than private traders do. Earlier to the formation of LAMPS forest department used to lease out forest areas to private contractors who in turn engaged tribal and non-tribal people to collect minor forest produces. Private contractors used to pay very low wages to MFP collectors, and these collectors were at the mercy of the traders. All this has changed overnight with the formation of LAMPS. Enquiries and the available data have revealed that LAMPS have been giving 60 per cent to 100 per cent more remuneration to MFP collectors than the private contractors did. For example, in the case of honey, tribal collectors used to get Rs. 25 per k.g. from the private contractors, whereas they are getting about Rs. 45 per k.g. from LAMPS at present. This is true with regard to other MFP items also. Again, the formation of LAMPS has induced a virtual competition in the MFP market. Owing to the existence of LAMPS, local traders have been quoting higher prices for the produce. Earlier, in the absence of LAMPS, and absence of competition thereto, local traders had the monopoly, and taking this advantage they had the usual tendency to quote very low prices and get away with the booty.

At this point a relevant question is to be unhesitatingly answered and that is whether the LAMPS have been engaging only their members and that too directly in MFP collection. The answer to this question is in the negative in the case of a large number of LAMPS. To our surprise it has been found that a number of LAMPS have engaged even tribal non-members for collection of MFP and in a few LAMPS contact between the society and members is completely lacking. They have engaged tribal collectors who act as middlemen between the society and members.

Thus, LAMPS have been able to provide better remuneration/wages to the MFP collectors than the private contractors were doing and have achieved significant gains in terms of earnings of revenues in different business activities they handle. But this economic performance is largely attributable to a very substantial amount of assistance provided by the government to LAMPS. Since their inception till 1998-99 the government had pumped in a total of Rs. 454.77 Lakhs into the LAMPS in Karnataka in the form of share capital, subsidy and loans. Economic performance of LAMPS, which is not very satisfactory at any standards has been at this enormous public cost.

It can be concluded with the observation that though the organisation of LAMPS has helped the tribal collectors in terms of their earnings, the gains are very much below their potential. Again, the earnings of tribal collectors are not consistent from year to year. Failure of LAMPS is also mirrored in the fact that many a non-member is also engaged in MFP collection which explains the reality that to that extent members are deprived of the opportunity to earn from this activity.

Social Performance

Social-performance can be assessed in terms of enrolment of members, percentage of actual members to potential members, participation of members in the activities and management of LAMPS and the quality of participation.

In terms of enrolment of members, the performance of LAMPS is very poor. Total tribal population in the area of operation of 21 LAMPS, i.e., in 21 talukas as per 1991 census is 2,58,747. A projection of 2 per cent increase in tribal population per annum will yield a total tribal population of 3,00,842 in 1999. Half of this population can be assumed as potential members which means participation of members in the activities of LAMPS is not much encouraging. In all the 21 LAMPS taken together only 42 per cent of the total members take part in collection and pooling of MFP. Among these members who are engaged in collection of MFP, the number of those who have direct relationship with the society as sellers of MFP is negligible. A large number of members sell the produce through the agents or middlemen engaged by the LAMPS. Thus, a majority of the members are actually unaware of their relationship with the society and their role in its progress.

Frequent visits paid by many members to the LAMPS should not be construed as their intimate relationship with and their involvement in the day-to-day affairs of the society. Enquiries have sufficiently revealed that a large section of the members frequent the LAMPS just in search of one or the other loan, as also to meet officials and other members who also happen to pay such visits.

It was found that members' knowledge of the activities of LAMPS is also very poor. They lack awareness about marketing of MFP, the role of LAMPS in tribal welfare etc. The only tribals who have good knowledge of activities of LAMPS are agents of these societies, i.e., the persons appointed by the LAMPS to procure MFP from forests. This speaks voluminously for failure of LAMPS as the arrangement of procuring MFP through agents is clear violation of the principle of co-operative business.

Members' involvement in the management of the society is also not satisfactory. On an average about 38 per cent of the total members in all the LAMPS taken together attended general body meetings. But if the case of individual societies is taken, attendance of members in general body meetings has been less than 15 per cent in a few societies.

Many presidents and directors of the board also do not possess reasonable knowledge of the activities and functions of the LAMPS. Their capability to take decisions is also poor. Thus, in many societies elected directors are easily carried away by the decisions of the officials. Enquiries and cross-questioning have revealed that only a handful of the elected directors are capable of decision making and have knowledge about co-operation and activities of LAMPS.

Thus, the performance of LAMPS in social sphere is dismal. They have failed to create sufficient awareness among members. They have not contributed to build managerial capability and decision making capacity among the tribals. On the contrary they contributed a lot to increase in economic inequalities among the members since the agents earn a good deal of money in the form of commission leaving the member content with the low price paid for the produce he collects.

Ecological Performance

Extraction of minor forest produces has a bearing on the ecosystem. Over harvesting of these products from trees and plants will affect their growth and hence ecological balance will be endangered. It has been observed that there has been a decline in forest cover over the years. The main reason for this is earmarking of a substantial portion of the forest area for national parks and sanctuaries. A decrease in forest cover and an increase in tribal population has caused tribals to depend upon lesser area of forests for extraction of MFP. Though the role of LAMPS in the destruction of ecosystem is not established, dependence of more number of tribals on the dwindling forest areas has its own contribution in aggravating ecological imbalance.

First, enquiries with ecologists, social activists and forest officials have revealed that MFP harvesting has gone beyond optimum level. Over harvesting affects environment, as it will have a worsening effect on animals, birds and forests. Over harvesting is with commercial motive. It is usually observed in the case of Amla (Emblica officinalis) and honey. In the case of Amla it is essential that about 20 percent of the produce should be left in the plant so that it will help regeneration. With overharvesting, plants and forests will dwindle and with a depleted forest cover and absence of many important types of plants in future, tribal life will be at danger. It is observed that only about 20 percent of the tribals are doing optimum level of harvesting.

Most unscientific method of harvesting is done in the case of honey. Only upper part of the beehive contains honey and it is advisable to cut only that part and extract honey from it. If that part of the beehive which does not contain honey is left unaffected it will help bees for further production of honey. Many a time fire is used to scare away bees to make it easy to extract honey. This will have a worsening effect on bee population and they will not be in a position to use the same tree to produce honey. If fire is not used to scare away the bees, they will be attracted to the same tree again and hence honey production will go on without any hindrances. Another thing usually noticed is that beehive is cut just methodically affecting the larvae and causing their death.

Declining species of Kudiamavu trees (Cinnamomum Sp.) is observed of late in Chamarajanagar and Yalandur talukas. Bark of this tree is used in agarbathi making. Tribal people agree that this decline is a result of their overharvest of the bark.

Second, harvesting should be done cautiously and in such a way as not to affect the branches. Instances are aplenty where tribals cut small branches of Amla tree while harvesting the produce. As a result, growth of the tree is stunted and quantity of produce will decline in future.

Third, parasites like orchids grow on some trees. It is necessary on the part of the harvestor of the produce to remove it so that further growth is made easy and its produce bearing capacity is enhanced. But this is rarely done by tribals.

In short, ecological performance of LAMPS is utterly poor. Though the role of MFP extraction activity in the destruction of ecosystem is not established, most unscientific method of harvesting of many products by tribals has definitely caused depletion of forest cover to some extent and also to decline in produce—bearing capacity of trees. Sustainable harvesting and scientific method of harvesting require a good deal of training to tribals. Enquiries and observations of this author have revealed that no LAMPS in Karnataka has so far done this exercise.It is a matter of pride to observe that Ashoka Trust for Research in Ecology and Environment of B. R. Hills, an organisation working for improvement in ecology and environment has involved many social activists and non-governmental organisations to train the tribals in scientific harvesting and sustainable level of harvesting of MFP.

Correlation Matrix

In order to know about the quantitative relationship between various parameters of LAMPS in Karnataka, a correlation matrix is worked out. The Same is presented. below.

Variables

X1 Membership
X2 Share Capital
X3 Reserves
X4 Deposits
X5 Borrowings
X6 Loans advanced

X7 Overdues
X8 Marketing
X9 Distribution
X10 Total Turnover
X11 Assets
X12 Liabilities
X13 Cost of administration
X14 Profits
X15 Losses

It may be observed from the matrix that excepting in the cases of variables X5 and X15, rest of the variables are strongly positively correlated. This indicates that there has been quantitative expansion with regard to these variables. Variable X5, which relates to borrowing, is strongly negatively correlated with all other variables excepting variable X15, which indicates losses. This is mainly due to the fact that borrowings are negligible in most of the LAMPS and marginal in the rest. The variable X15 which indicates losses, is also strongly negatively correlated with the rest of the variables. This is due to the fact that losses have fluctuated over the years.

The whole thing that can be summarily said is that, most of the variables have witnessed quantitative expansion between 1990-91 and 1998-99. The actual data relating to these variables is presented in Appendix 1. The qualitative aspect is already explained in the earlier part of this chapter. In fact it is the qualitative variables such as organisation, management, social and ecological performance which have contributed to the poor performance of LAMPS rather than the quantitative variables. This fact is vindicated further in the next chapter through case studies.

Karnataka State LAMPS Federation

Karnataka State LAMPS Federation has come into existence in the year 1998 with a view to coordinate the

CORRELATION MATRIX (ZERO IS DEPENDENT VARIABLE)

	X1	X2	X3	X4	X5	X6	X7	X8	X9	X10	X11	X12	X13	X14	X15
X1	1.00	0.95	0.97	0.80	–.77	0.81	0.93	0.79	0.96	0.92	0.98	0.94	0.80	0.87	0.76
X2	0.95	1.00	0.98	0.91	–.71	0.91	0.82	0.85	0.95	0.99	0.98	0.99	0.90	0.97	–.83
X3	0.97	0.98	1.00	0.91	–.77	0.88	0.85	0.79	0.94	0.96	0.98	0.96	0.91	0.94	–.79
X4	0.80	0.91	0.91	1.00	–.75	.95	0.62	0.68	0.79	0.91	0.89	0.85	0.96	0.88	–.71
X5	–.77	–.71	–.77	–.75	1.00	–.63	–.57	–.39	–.61	–.67	–.79	–.64	–.77	–.63	0.57
X6	0.81	0.91	0.88	0.96	–.63	1.00	0.68	0.75	0.86	0.93	0.90	0.87	0.86	0.86	–.68
X7	0.93	0.82	0.85	0.68	–.57	0.68	1.00	0.75	0.93	0.80	0.88	0.83	0.61	0.69	–.59
X8	0.79	0.85	0.79	0.68	–.39	0.75	0.75	1.00	0.87	0.90	0.80	0.87	0.65	0.85	–.56
X9	0.96	0.95	0.94	0.79	–.61	0.86	0.93	0.87	1.00	0.94	0.96	0.95	0.76	0.87	–.73
X10	0.92	0.99	0.96	0.91	–.67	0.93	0.80	0.90	0.94	1.00	0.96	0.97	0.89	0.96	–.75
X11	0.98	0.98	0.98	0.89	–.79	0.90	0.88	0.80	0.96	0.96	1.00	0.95	0.86	0.90	–.74
X12	0.94	0.99	0.96	0.85	–.64	0.87	0.83	0.87	0.95	0.97	0.95	1.00	0.86	0.96	–.87
X13	0.80	0.90	0.91	0.96	–.77	0.86	0.61	0.65	0.76	0.89	0.86	0.86	1.00	0.90	–.82
X14	0.87	0.97	0.94	0.88	–.63	0.86	0.69	0.85	0.87	0.96	0.90	0.96	0.90	1.00	–.83
X15	–.76	–.83	–.79	–.71	0.57	–.68	–.59	–.56	–.73	–.75	–.74	–.87	–.82	–.83	1.00

working of all the LAMPS in the state. It started functioning on 15.8.1998. At present 20 LAMPS are its members. Muthathi LAMPS has not yet enrolled as member of this federation. The Federation has a share capital of Rs. 3. 39 Lakhs. Karnataka LAMPS Federation is the first of its kind in the entire country.

The Federation has come into being with the main objectives of co-ordinating the working of LAMPS in the state, providing better prices for minor forest products by arranging marketing facilities and undertaking or promoting on its own or on behalf of its members inter-state or international trade.

The Federation has an elected President. It has a Deputy Registrar of Co-operative Societies as its Chief Executive. It is head quartered at Mysore.

The Federation has commenced its business of purchasing MFP from member LAMPS and selling them. To start with, it is selling the products to TRIFED, New Delhi, which has one of its regional offices at Bangalore. The Federation has signed a Memorandum of understanding with the TRIFED on 23. 4. 1999 for marketing of minor forest produce. It has procured about 120 metric tonnes of soapnut and antuwala from LAMPS and has sold it to TRIFED.

In 1998-99 Government of Karnataka had sanctioned Rs. 5.00 Lakhs to the Federation for infrastructure facility and the Government of India had sanctioned Rs. 3.00 Lakhs in the form of share capital.

The Federation has planned to take up procurement of minor forest produces on a large scale and to set up processing plants.

The Role Played by the State Government

The Government of Karnataka has come out in a big

measure to help the LAMPS. It has been extending financial assistance to them in different ways every year.

The state government has implemented a scheme to provide education and training to the tribal members of all the LAMPS in the state. This scheme has been in vogue since 1986. This is being done through Karnataka State Co-operative Federation. At present there are four teachers to impart training and education and they are based at district co-operative unions of Mysore, Madikeri, Chikmagalur and Mangalore. Education and Training in the fields of collection of minor forest produces, basket making, coir making etc., are provided to tribals. This has helped a lot to increase skill among the tribals. An officer of the rank of Deputy Registrar of Co-operative Societies is serving as Project Officer for LAMPS of State Co-operative Federation. The programme of education and training of tribals is under his supervision.

Critical Evaluation of the Working of LAMPS in Karnataka

Since the establishment of the first LAMPS in Karnataka i. e., 1965 till 2002, LAMPS have really made rapid strides in the field of tribal development. From three LAMPS in 1967, their number has increased to 21 by 1994. Membership in them has found an increase on a large scale and activities undertaken by them have also gone up voluminously. Majority of the LAMPS in Karnataka have left their indelible mark in social and economic life of the tribals. They have been able to undertake may activities such as collection and sale of minor forest produce, distribution of rationed articles, sale of consumer goods and agricultural inputs, supplies of consumer articles and food grains to designated institutions such as hostels and tribal welfare centres, and imparting training under vocations to many of their members.

Some LAMPS deserve special mention for having gone a step further and for having undertaken special activities such as processing and banking. Four LAMPS are at present doing the activity of processing of minor forest produces and five LAMPS have taken up banking activities in the same way as commercial banks and co—operative banks do. Many LAMPS have really made a dent in tribal life.

There has been a quantitative and qualitative improvement in the working of LAMPS in Karnataka. In the year of establishment of each LAMPS, it started functioning with just a hundreds of members and had a turnover of just five to ten thousand rupees. At present every LAMPS is having a turnover of lakhs of rupees.

It is true that LAMPS have been able to create a large number of employment opportunities for MFP collectors as also in their offices for clerical and sales work. Contribution of LAMPS in the field of tribal empowerment cannot be underestimated. It is a credit to LAMPS that they have been able to reduce the role of middlemen to a large extent.

But seen from the other side, the performance of LAMPS does not paint a rosy picture. Their economic performance is mixed. It is true that LAMPS in Karnataka have been able to provide employment opportunities to a large number of tribal people and to enhance income earning capacity among them. But the bad state of affairs is that in some LAMPS, even non-members are allowed to collect and sell MFP and there has been no virtual link between the society and the member. Instead, tribal agents collect MFP from members and sell them to the LAMPS.

More than half of the total number of LAMPS in Karnataka have earned accumulated profits. A large number of LAMPS have earned profits in majority of the years. But only a few LAMPS have declared dividend on the shares of members only for some years. Thus strictly speaking, these societies are not really following the principle of co-operative business.

In social sphere the performance LAMPS is dismal. Actual membership to potential members is far less. Total tribal population in 1999 in the area of operation of 21 LAMPS is 2,99,790 and hence potential members are 1,49,895. But the actual membership is 64,118. Thus actual membership is only 42.9 per cent of potential members. Participation of members in the activities and meetings of LAMPS is also very poor.

Ecological performance of LAMPS is not praiseworthy. Optimum level of harvesting and sustainable harvesting are the important requirements to maintain ecological balance and to let the plants and species grow for the future. But the sordid thing is LAMPS have not thought of imparting training to tribals on these lines. MFP harvesting is being done only with commercial motive.

REFERENCES

1. Government of Karnataka, Department of Tribal Welfare, Tribal Sub-plan, Annual Plan—1999—2000, p. 6.

CHAPTER — 4

CASE STUDIES OF LAMPS

In the previous chapter a general view of progress of Large-sized Adivasi Multi-purpose Co-operative Societies in Karnataka has been obtained. In order to accurately assess the performance of these societies before drawing several conclusions regarding LAMPS, it is found important to analyse in depth some more factors involved in the working of some of these societies. Business expansion activities of LAMPS, nature of and causes for the problems the LAMPS are facing, and notable reasons for heavy losses have to be studied in detail. This exercise has been undertaken in this chapter.

Of the 21 LAMPS in Karnataka State, eight of these societies have been taken for case studies. These societies are carefully selected out of the 12 LAMPS which the author had personally visited during the course of the present study to collect primary data and to elicit information. The eight LAMPS are Hunsur and Heggadadevanakote in Mysore district, Chamarajanagar and B.R. Hills in Chamarajanagar district, Basavanahalli in Coorg District, Mudigere in Chickmagalur district, Udupi in Udupi district and Muthathi in Mandya district. These

LAMPS have been selected from six out of the eight districts where they exist.

Many criteria were taken into consideration to select LAMPS for case studies. The first criterion has been dependence of LAMPS on forests. The societies have been selected in such a way as to include both heavily forest-dependent and slightly forest-dependent. The societies which are heavily forest-dependant are Heggadadevanakote, Chamrajanagara, B.R. Hills and Mudigere. The other four societies which are not heavily forest-dependent are Hunsur, Basavanahalli, Udupi and Muthathi. Selection of the societies on this basis will help to analyse the role of minor forest produces in the performance of LAMPS and the problems thereon.

Accumulated profit and loss position h as been another criterion considered. Of the eleven LAMPS which were successful in garnering accumulated profits as on 31.3.1999, six LAMPS are taken up for case studies. They include a few societies which have a very high amount of profits such as Chamarajanagar and also a very low amount of profits such as B.R. Hills. And the remaining four LAMPS fall between these two extremes. They are LAMPS of Basavanahalli, Mudigere, Udupi and Muthathi. Of the nine LAMPS which have incurred accumulated losses as on 31.3.1999, two were selected for case studies. They include Hunsur which had a staggering amount of accumulated losses and Heggadadevanakote which had a not so high amount of accumulated losses.

Processing is an activity which has the potentiality of yielding very high profit margins by way of adding value to the commodity. Only a few LAMPS have been able to take up that activity. Banking is another activity which has been ventured upon by a few LAMPS in recent years.

Some LAMPS have tried for some time, or still doing, other income generating activities such as nursery seedling, coir making, basket making, candle making and brick making. Udupi and Basavanahalli LAMPS have set up a carpentry unit of their own. All these factors have been taken into account and performance of LAMPS in these activities is tested in the course of case studies.

In the area of operation of some LAMPS, we find non-governmental organisations with a missionary zeal and working for tribal welfare. LAMPS of B.R. Hills and Heggadadevanakote have been selected for case studies mainly with this background. There are two important voluntary organisations operating one at B.R. Hills and the other in Heggadadevanakote taluka. The idea is to assess the performance of LAMPS in these areas and the influence of these voluntary organisations on tribals and on the working of LAMPS.

It is generally said that people of some districts possess a strong co-operative character. It is so said of Coorg and South Kanara districts. The present Coorg district was earlier known as Coorg State and South Kanara district earlier belonged to erstwhile Madras Presidency. The present Udupi district belonged to South Kanara district until it was bifurcated and made a separate district in 1998. To test the general belief of co-operative character, one society in Coorg district and one society in the erstwhile south Kanara district have been taken.

LAMPS Udupi has been selected to cover the coastal districts of South Kanara and Udupi.

Muthathi LAMPS in Mandya district has been taken up as it is the only LAMPS outside the ITDP area and which has found its existence just five years ago and which is one of the latest societies to be organised among the 21 LAMPS that exist in Karnataka.

Success or failure of LAMPS in general, their service to the members and their contribution to tribal welfare, are analysed at the end of the chapter.

We shall begin the exercise of case studies of different LAMPS by taking a view of general aspects such as forest area leased out to each LAMPS, their profit and loss position and different income earning activities undertaken by them.

The Table 4.1 shows the forest area leased to each of eight LAMPS in acres. The figures reveal that the LAMPS of Hunsur, Basavanahalli, Udupi and Muthathi are not heavily dependent on forests whereas the other four LAMPS heavily depend on forests. Only three LAMPS i.e., Basavanahalli, Mudigere and Udupi have undertaken special activities. Of these, LAMPS of Basavanahalli and Mudigere have taken up processing activity, whereas Mudigere and Udupi LAMPS are pursuing banking activities. Basavanahalli and Udupi LAMPS have set up carpentry training units.

LAMPS of Hunsur and Heggadadevanakote are working under accumulated losses as on 31.3.1999 and the other six societies have accumulated profits to their credit.

Table 4.2 shows the number of elected and ex-officio directors of each of the eight LAMPS and also whether the President is a tribal or an officer. It is amply indicated that Presidents of four societies are officers belonging to forest department.

1. LAMPS, HUNSUR

Hunsur is one of the talukas of Mysore district. It is also a sub-divisional head quarters which covers four talukas. Hunsur and its adjoining taluka Periyapatna have a large chunk of tribal population and vast stretches of plain areas. Though the forests have been depleted over the years, the region still has large pockets covered by woods.

The Large-sized Adivasi Multi-purpose Co-operative Society, Hunsur was registered under state co-operative

Table 4.1

Forest Area, Special Activities and Accumulated Profit and Loss Position of Selected LAMPS in Karnataka

Sl. No.	*Name of the LAMPS*	*Forest area leased to LAMPS (Acres)*	*Special Activity undertaken*	*Accumulated*	
				Profit (Rs. in Lakhs)	*Loss*
1	LAMPS, Hunsur	02,200	–	–	8.48
2	LAMPS, Heggadadevanakote	15,470	–	–	2.19
3	LAMPS, Chamarajanagar	60,59	–	23.92	–
4	LAMPS, B.R. Hills	24,000	–	0.10	–
5	LAMPS, Basávanahalli	7,286	Processing and Carpentry	1.59	–
6	LAMPS, Mudigere	19,000	Banking and Processing	0.44	–
7	LAMPS, Udupi	11,574	Banking and Carpentry	1.54	–
8	LAMPS, Muthathi	1,740	–	3.45	–

Sources: Data personally collected from the societies.

Table 4.2

Presidents and Directors of Selected LAMPS

Sl. No.	*Name of the LAMPS*	*President*	*Number of directors*	
			Elected	*Ex-Officio*
1	LAMPS, Hunsur	DCF	06	05
2	LAMPS, Heggadadevanakote	Tribal	06	05
3	LAMPS, Chamarajanagar	DCF	06	05
4	LAMPS, B.R. Hills	ACF	06	05
5	LAMPS, Basavanahalli	Tribal	08	03
6	LAMPS, Mudigere	Tribal	06	05
7	LAMPS, Udupi	Trible	09	02
8	LAMPS, Muthathi	DCF	07	04

Source: Data personally collected from the societies.

societies Act on 24.3.1971. It commenced business after a lapse of about two months since registration. In the beginning it was named as Labour contract Multi-Purpose Society. After introduction of the tribal sub-plan the society was renamed as LAMPS. This society has got two talukas-Hunsur and Periyapatna in its area of operation.

The society has 21 objectives as enshrined in its byelaw adopted for governance. Its broad objectives include providing credit facilities to members, to supply consumer articles to tribal welfare centres and hostels, to take up processing activity, to undertake activities like lift irrigation and dairying in the name of the society, to develop thrift, self help and economic discipline among the members, and to assist members to build residential houses.

Membership

Number of tribal families living in the area of operation is 4600. The division between Hunsur and Periyapatna talukas is 3412 and 1188 families respectively. According to 1991 census, Hunsur taluka has got a tribal population of 23,457. This is about 10.5 percent of the total population of the taluka of 2,22,173. Periyapatna taluka has got a tribal population of 6,483 which is about 3.43 percent of the total population of the taluka of 1,88,902. The society has a membership of 6,431 as on 31.3.2002.

Membership and share capital in Hunsur LAMPS in some selected years is shown in the following table.

The table depicts that membership in the LAMPS has remained stagnant between 1994-95 and 1998-99 at 6,421. And it had remained the same between 1990-91 and 1993-94. It has been found that membership in the LAMPS has not increased substantially since 1990-91.

Viewed from another angle, that is total tribal population and potential members, the society has fared badly. The society in its area of operation has a total tribal population of 29,940. Projection of 2 percent increase in population per annum will yield a total population of 35,600. Fifty percent of this population can be viewed as potential members, i.e., persons who could have been admitted into the society as members. In that sense, actual membership in the LAMPS should have been more than 17,800. It can be easily assessed that either the LAMPS has failed to enrol more number of members by canvassing its existence, or it has not shown keen interest in admitting new members, or tribal people have shown reluctance to enrol as members of LAMPS and to avail the facilities.

Table 4.3

Membership and Share Capital in Selected Years

Sl. No.	*Years*	*Number of Members*	*Share Capital (in Rupees)*
1.	1990-91	2,025	5,52,048.25
2.	1993-94	2,025	5,52,048.25
3.	1994-95	6,421	5,63,568.25
4.	1995-96	6,421	8,14,813.25
5.	1998-99	6,421	13,09,000.00
6.	2001-02	6,431	14,38,000.00

Source: Data personally collected from the society.

All the members of Hunsur LAMPS belong to non-hill tribes category. They are mainly of two sub-sects, namely Jenu Kuruba and Betta Kuruba.

The society has a share capital of Rs. 13.09 Lakhs as on 31.3.1999. Of this, share capital from members was Rs. 2.29 lakhs and of government was Rs. 10.80 Lakhs. The percentage of members' share and government's share in the total share capital base of the society is 17.5 and 82.5 percent respectively. This fact is clear enough to show that the society has very largely depended on the government for economic assistance. In the absence of governmental assistance, the society is not able to muster sufficient funds and to provide services to members in true spirit.

Bye-laws of the society, many provisions of which were recently amended, provide for obtaining Rs. 100 as share capital from each member at the time of his enrolment. If the bye-law provisions are given effect to, the society should have been able to mobilise Rs. 6,42,100.00 as share capital from members. But its total share capital from members is just Rs. 2.29 lakhs. The value of each share was Rs.10 in the beginning and a large number of members have not paid the remaining amount of Rs. 90 to be eligible members even after amendment of the bye-law to this effect. This explains the fact of very poor share base in the society.

Only 132 members of this LAMPS i.e., just about two percent of the total members have become members in others credit societies in its area of operation.

Management

The committee of management of the society consists of eleven directors. Of this, six directors are elected from among the members. The remaining five are ex-officio directors. They are Deputy Conservator of Forest, Block Development officer, Tahsildar, Integrated Tribal Development Plan Programme officer and a nominee of the District Central Co-operative Bank.

The society has an official President in the Deputy Conservator of Forests, Hunsur division. It has a paid Secretary as its Chief Executive.

Business Activities

One of the important activities undertaken by Hunsur LAMPS is collection and sale of minor forest produces. Its total business transactions in minor forest produces were Rs. 1.23 lakhs in 1996-97, Rs. 9.29 lakhs in 1997-98 and Rs. 2.39 Lakhs in 1998-99. The figures show that there is no consistency and continuously upward trend in the earnings of the society from minor forest produces business. Depletion in the forest area and reduced harvesting because of lack of availability of produces are the important reasons for this phenomenon. Most of the forest area in Hunsur Taluka is earmarked as national park and hence two range areas have been taken out of business jurisdiction of the LAMPS.

Another important, of course, the major business of this LAMPS is consumer business, i.e., sale of essential articles and consumer goods. This business had a transaction of Rs. 5.71 Lakhs in 1996-97, Rs. 4.02 Lakhs in 1997-98 and Rs. 3.50 Lakhs in 1998-99. This indicates in some years, the volume of this business exceeded that of minor forest produces.

Some years earlier, the LAMPS had the business of making supplies of essential commodities and consumer articles to hostels in Hunsur taluka. But this business has not been entrusted to it for the last five years. At present this business had been entrusted to other agencies. Hence the LAMPS has lost one important activity which it was performing earlier.

The LAMPS had taken up other activities such as developing and sale of nursery plants and coir making. These two activities were performed only for a few years and they have been given up in the last two years. Lack of skill on the part of LAMPS to do these activities was the main reason why they were given up.

Thus, LAMPS Hunsur is at present engaged in only two types of business, i.e., minor forest produces business and consumer business. Both these are non-credit varieties of business. The LAMPS has not taken up any credit activity.

Table 4.4

Profitability in Business

Year	*MFP Sales*	*Laese Money Paid*	*Sale of Consumer Goods*	*Purchases of Consumer Goods*
1990-91	1,28,000	70,000	1,96,000	1,83,000
1991-92	1,68,000	93,500	2,08,000	1,93,000
1992-93	1,69,500	93,50	2,12,000	1,97,600
1994-95	1,84,000	98,750	2,31,000	2,14,000
1998-99	2,39,000	1,25,000	3,50,000	3,27,000

Source: Data personally collected from the society.

Figures in the Table 4.4 indicate that both MFP activity and consumer business activity of LAMPS have yielded profits in all the select years. For MFP business, the profit margin works out to be an average of about 45 percent in select years. The society has earned a profit of about 7 to 8 percent in consumer business.

Financial Assistance by the Government

The society has availed various types of financial assistance from the government. This can be seen in table 4.5.

Thus the society has availed financial assistance from the government to the tune of Rs. 22,68,000. Of this Rs. 15,80,000 has been loan and share capital and Rs. 6,88,000 has been subsidy of various types.

Table 4.6 indicates that 62 percent of the members of LAMPS are agricultural labourers who are landless. Only 38 percent of the members own land. Twenty five percent of the members were owning less than 2 acres of land each. Thus about 87 percent of the total members are

Table 4.5

Government's Financial Assistance

(Amount in Rupees)

Sl. No.	*Schemes for which Assistance was availed*	*Amount of Loan and Share Capital*	*Amount of Subsidy*
1.	Share capital	4,70,500	–
2.	Margin money	–	50,000
3.	Working capital loan	5,00,500	–
4.	Lease Amount Subsidy	–	2,15,000
5.	Business Loan	26,000	–
6.	Loans for Retail outlets	1,60,000	–
7.	Subsidy for Retail outlets	–	40,000
8.	Loan for Firewood Depot	35,000	–
9.	Subsidy for Firewood Depot	–	15,000
10.	Managerial Subsidy	–	71,000
11.	Additional Share Loan	75,000	–
12.	Subsidy for honey processing unit	–	1,62,000
13.	Building Loan	3,13,000	–
14.	Subsidy for tamarind processing unit	–	1,00,000
15.	Subsidy for Miscellaneous expenditure	–	35,000
	Total	**15,80,000**	**6,88,000**

Source: Data Personally Collected from the society.

agricultural labourers and marginal farmers. This had reduced the potentiality of LAMPS to advance agricultural credit to its members as the quantum of demand for loan is very much limited.

Table 4.6

Membership According to Land Holdings

Sl. No.	*Particulars*	*No. of Members*	*Percentage*
1.	Agricultural Labourers	3,981	62
2.	Less than 1 acre	836	13
3.	1 to 2 acres	770	12
4.	2 to 5 acres	770	12
5.	Above 5 acres	64	01
	Total	**6,421**	**100**

Source: Data personally collected from the society.

The table 4.7 indicates that the society had a paid up share capital amount of Rs. 13.09 Lakhs and it had an accumulated loss of Rs. 8.48 Lakhs as on 31.3.1999.

An Assessment of the Working of the Society

Eventhough LAMPS Hunsur is one of the earliest of such societies to be established in Karnataka State, its performance even after nearly three decades of its existence is anything but satisfactory. Actual membership in the society is far less than potential members in its area of operation. Efforts are not made to increase membership. The business activities of the society are very limited, they being only MFP activity and consumer business. It has miserably failed to take up non-credit activities such as banking and advancing term loans.

The society had a staggering amount of accumulated loss to the extent of Rs. 8.48 Lakhs. It is yet to recover Rs. 65,000 of its amount misappropriated by two former salesmen. The society has taken recourse to legal action to recover the money.

Table 4.7

Financial Position as on 31.3.1999

	Liabilities	*Amount in Rupees*		*Assets*	*Amount in Rupees*
1.	Paid up share capital	13,09,000	1.	Cash on hand	176
2.	Reserve Fund	6,912	2.	Bank Accounts	3,07,971
3.	Other Funds	66,412	3.	Deposits	42,800
4.	Deposits	43,740	4.	Loans from Members	43,647
5.	Loan from Government	5,00,000	5.	Movable and Immovable properties	5,10,143
6.	Subsidy by Government	6,88,000	6.	Closing stock	8,63,500
7.	Reserves	67,173	7.	Loss	8,48,000
			8.	Recovery Accounts	65,000
	Total	**26,81,237**		**Total**	**26,81,237**

Source: Data Personally Collected from the Society.

The LAMPS had suffered a heavy loss in MFP revenues as the forest area leased out to it has shrunk in size because of earmarking of the area as national park. It is true that this is one important reason for poor performance of the LAMPS. Expansion of business activities can definitely go a long way in helping the society to perform better.

2. LAMPS, CHAMARAJANAGAR

Chamarajanagar is one of the districts in Karnataka State. It was a taluka of undivided Mysore district till 1998

Fig. 4.1

Capital Structure of Hunsur Lamps 1998-99

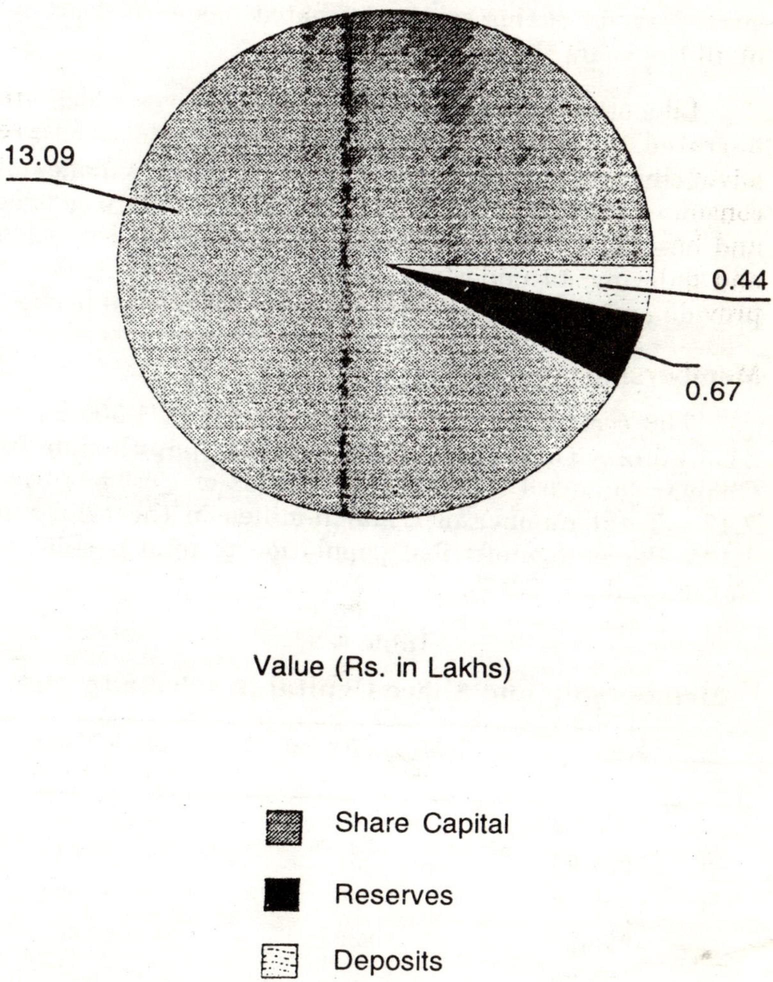

in which year it was made a separate district. The region is known for vast stretches of hilly and forest areas.

Chamarajanagar LAMPS was registered on 20.11.1978 and it commenced business about four months later. Novelty of this society is that it has earned profits in all the years since its inception.

Like other LAMPS, it has got 21 objectives which are narrated in its bye-laws. Its prominent objectives are advancing credit to tribal members, to make supplies of consumer articles and food grains to tribal welfare centres and hostels, to undertake activities such as lift irrigation and dairying, to undertake public works contract and to provide assistance to members to build residential houses.

Membership

The society had a total membership of 1,300 as on 31.3.2002. Total scheduled tribes population in Chamarajanagara taluka as per census of 1991 has been 7,175. Total number of tribal families in the taluka is 1,125. Percentage of tribal population to total population in the taluka is 2.3.

Table 4.8

Membership and Share Capital in selected years

Sl. No.	*Year*	*No. of Members*	*Share Capital (in Rupees)*
1.	1978-79	600	1,06,000
2.	1994-95	955	4,29,640
3.	1995-96	1,230	7,31,970
4.	1996-97	1,230	8,55,000
5.	1997-98	1,230	8,55,000
6.	1998-99	1,270	8,55,000
7.	2001-02	1,300	14,49,000

Source: Data personally collected from the society.

Table 4.8 shows that the society started with a modest membership of 600. Over the years it has marginally risen and stands at just 1,300 in 2001-02. Its membership was stagnant at 1,230 between 1995-96 and 1997-98.

Tribal population in Chamrajanagara taluka at present is around 8,725, considering about 2 percent increase per annum since 1991 when the last census was taken. Of this, fifty percent of the population, i.e., 4,363 persons can be viewed as potential members. If the society had made earnest efforts a large chunk of this population could have been admitted as members of the society. At present its membership stands at less than 25 percent of potential membership.

All the members of the LAMPS are of hill tribe category and they belong to Soliga community. No member of this society has enrolled as a member of any credit society in the area of operation.

The society has share capital of the amount of Rs. 8,55,000 as on 31.3.1999. Of this, share capital of members is Rs. 45,000 and that of the government is Rs. 8,10,000. This again explains undue dependence of the society on the government. Out of the total amount of share capital, the percentage of members, share and government's share works out to be 5.3 and 94.7 respectively.

Management

At present the society has 11 directors on its committee of management. Six directors are elected from among tribal members and the remaining five are ex-officio directors. They are Block Development Officer, Tahsildar, nominee of the Mysore district Central Co-operative Bank, integrated tribal development programme officer and Agricultural Officer. President of the society is not an elected member. Instead, Deputy Conservator of Forests,

Chamarajanagar division is working as President of the society.

The post of the Secretary is held by a co-operative development officer. His services are lent to the society by the department of Co-operation for a certain period. He has been drawing salary and emoluments out of the funds of the society.

Business Activities

LAMPS, Chamarajanagara is engaged in only three activities. They are, (i) collection and sale of minor forest produces, (ii) consumer business, and (iii) supply of food grains and consumer articles to tribal welfare centres and hostels. It has got four retail outlets through which rationed articles and non-controlled goods are sold.

The society has no processing unit and has not embarked upon any processing activity. Activities such as brick making, basket making etc., which can help to provide job opportunities and training to people have not found place at any time in the society. It has not taken up banking activity too.

Thus, the society is engaged only in non-credit activities. Its major activities are collection and sale of minor forest produce and sale of consumer articles. The following table indicates margin of profits or otherwise in different items of business the society has taken up.

Table 4.9 depicts that the society has earned a profit of Rs. 8,65,596 in 1990-91, Rs. 11,69,443 in 1994-95, Rs. 6,40,000 in 1996-97 and Rs. 25,02,000 in 1998-99 in MFP activity. The society has been able to earn a profit margin of 7 to 8 percent in sale of consumer articles and of about 9 to 10 percent in the business of supplies of food grains and other articles to designated institutions.

Table 4.9

Profitability in Business

(Amount in Rupees)

Sl. No.	Year	MFP Sales	Lease Money paid	Sale of Consumer Goods	Purchase of Consumer Goods	Sale of Other Articles	Purchase of Other articles
1	1990-91	8,92,596	27,000	12,16,000	11,18,720	82,000	74,685
2	1994-95	12,14,443	45,000	21,04,000	19,56,960	6,30,000	5,67,000
3	1996-97	8,18,000	1,78,000	35,56,000	29,96,115	14,08,000	12,81,875
4	1998-99	28,02,000	3,00,000	12,96,000	11,92,320	95,000	86,450

Source: Data personally collected from the society.

Financial Assistance by the Government

The society has availed various types of financial assistance from the government. This is indicated in the table 4.10.

Table 4.10

Government's Financial Assistance

(Amount in Rupees)

Sl. No.	Schemes for which Assistance was availed	Amount of Loan and Share Capital	Amount of Subsidy
1.	Share capital	8,10,000	–
2.	Managerial subsidy	–	23,400
3.	Loan for Retail outlets	1,20,000	–
4.	Subsidy for retail outlets	–	30,000
5.	Lease Amount Subsidy	–	1,40,000
6.	Loan for godown construction	1,20,000	–
7.	Subsidy for honey processing unit	–	12,500
8.	Additional Share loan	1,50,000	–
9.	Working capital loan	2,00,000	–
10.	Building Loan	86,000	–
11.	Subsidy for Miscellaneous Expenditure	–	1,37,100
	Total	**14,86,000**	**3,43,000**

Source: Data Personally Collected from the society.

Table 4.11 depicts that 1,135 members i.e., 49.21 percent of the total members of the society are agricultural labourers. In other words, landless agricultural labourers are in overwhelming majority in the total number of members. 266 members have land less than 1 acre each and 151 members have land between 1 and 2 acres each. That means 1,042 members or 82.03 percent of the total members are agricultural labourers, and marginal farmers. Only 118 members or 9.29 percent of the total members

Table 4.11

Membership According to Land holdings

Sl. No.	*Particulars*	*No. of Members*	*Percentage*
1.	Agricultural labourers	625	49.21
2.	Less than 1 acre	266	20.94
3.	1 to 2 acres	151	11.88
4.	2 to 5 acres	118	9.29
5.	Above 5 acres	110	8.66
	Total	**1,270**	**100.00**

Source: Data personally collected from the society.

own more than 2 acres and less than 5 acres each. This includes 10 members who own coffee plantations of about 3 acres each. 110 members or 8.66 percent own land above 5 acres each which includes 8 members each of whom own about 6 acres of Coffee Plantation.

Financial Position

Prominent sources of finances of the society are share capital contributed by individual members and the government, reserve and other funds created out of net profit and loans and subsidy by the government. A picture of the financial position of the society as on 31.3.1999 can be had from the following table.

Problems Faced by the Society

After an indepth study into the working of the society and discussions with its office bearers and members, it was noticed that the society is facing many problems which are narrated hereunder.

1. Every time the lease amount is enhanced by the forest department. Some times it becomes unbearable on the part of the society.

Table 4.12

Financial position as on 31.3.1999

Liabilities	*Amount in Rupees*	*Assets*	*Amount in Rupees*
1. Paid up share capital	8,10,000	1. Cash Balance	08
2. Reserve Fund	20,23,796	2. bank Accounts	29,66,582
3. Loan and Subsidy from the Government	3,50,380	3. Investments	11,28,900
4. Employees' Security Deposit	37,900	4. Movable and Immovable properties	2,67,853
5. Reserve for stock deficit	1,36,504	5. Loans to be recovered	1,06,831
6. Interest on Deposits	30,000	6. Advances and other recoveries	10,19,232
7. Net Profit	23,92,390	7. Closing Stock	2,91,564
Total	**57,80,970**		**57,80,970**

Source: Data personally collected from the society.

2. There is a little delay in the grant of lease to the society by the forest department. During the gap period of lapse of earlier lease and grant of the new lease, the society cannot harvest minor forest produces. The society is forced to lose a huge amount of revenues because of this.

3. Unauthorised collection of minor forest produces by non-tribals and private contractors has caused erosion of revenues for the society and loss of income and employment on the part of the members.

4. Advance money for collection of minor forest produces is given to tribal collection agents. There

Fig. 4.2

Capital Structure of Chamarajanagara Lamps 1998-99

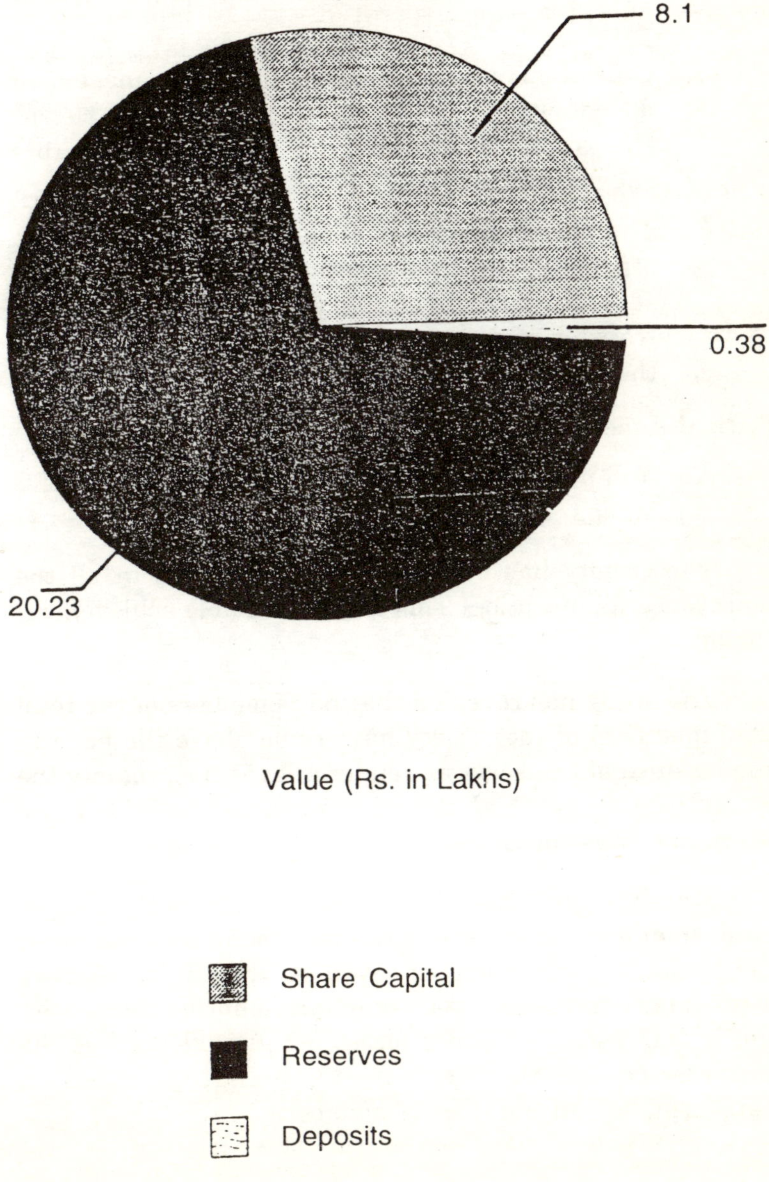

are cases where these agents have not procured produce for the society or have procured less than the value of the advance money taken. The society has lost nearly Rs. 2.5 Lakhs on this count.

5. Official members of the committee of management do not attend board meetings regularly. Hence, the society is deprived of their valuable suggestions.

6. The post of Secretary of the society is held by an officer of the Co-operation Department whose services are hired by the society. Frequent transfer of secretary is affecting the working of the society.

Critical Assessment of the Working of the Society

An indepth analysis of the working of LAMPS Chamarajanagar provides a mixed picture.

The society has been able to earn profits in all the years since its inception. This is a remarkable achievement indeed.

The study has revealed that 550 members of the total 1270 members of the society have come above the poverty line because of the services rendered by it, i.e., mainly the avenue the society had shown to members to collect and sell minor forest produces.

Members of the society have been able to get employment for about seven to eight months in the year. Again, not only the member, even all the adult members of his family have been getting employment as they assist him in harvesting of minor forest produces. Here lies the importance of the society in bringing about a transformation in the lives of members.

But there is no reason to take pride only on these factors. The working of the society viewed from a number of other factors provides a dismal picture.

Members in this society can be categorised into three groups from the view point of nature of their functioning and status. The first group consists of members who collect minor forest produces to earn wages. The second group of members work as middlemen or collection agents. There are 18 such agents in the society. They collect minor forest produces harvested by the members and bring them to the collection centres. The third type of members include those who are not engaged in minor forest produces business but get loans and subsidises from the society. These are affluent members who own land.

The above analysis gives a clear picture that a large number of members do not have a contact with the society. They sell the produce to the middlemen who in turn sell it to the society. This is virtually against the principles of co-operation. Members are working just as wage-earners and middlemen have been able to earn a huge amount of profits in the business.

Majority of the members are not aware of the nature of working of the society, their role in the society and the benefits they can obtain from it. They are under the impression that the LAMPS is an organ of the government.

It has been found that many non-tribals also collect minor forest produces and sell them to the society. Middlemen are allowed to collect the produce from any person and to pass it on to the society. Thus, the spirit of co-operation and the value of membership have been rendered useless.

The society has not been able to increase its membership significantly over the years. As explained in the beginning, less than 25 per cent of the potential members have been enrolled as actual members. The society has failed to canvass its usefulness and to take the tribal people into its fold.

The fact that even non-members can collect and sell minor forest produce, a privilege that is reserved only to the members, explains why a large chunk of tribals have not bothered to get themselves admitted as members of the society.

It has been ordained by the Karnataka State Co-operation department that only the elected tribal person can become president of the LAMPS. The same principle is enshrined in the model bye-law adopted by all the LAMPS. But this principle is deliberately given a go by and Deputy Conservator of forests, i.e., a high ranking officer of the forest department, is made president in this society. It is argued that such an arrangement will help the society to reap the benefits to the maximum extent. The argument putforth is that with the help of the officer-President, passes can be obtained for tribal collectors to enter the forests even early in the morning and late in the evening which is not possible if a tribal were to be in the saddle. It is said that forest officials allow people and vehicles to transport minor forest produces even at untimely hours at the behest of the DCF. In this way the principle of co-operation and tribal empowerment have suffered a great deal.

The society had performed credit activity in only one year. It advanced medium term loans to 13 members from the funds of DCC Bank for purchase of cart and bullock in 1993-94. Total amount of loan advanced was Rs. 75,000.00. No member repaid the loan and after a lapse of three years the loan became overdue. The society repaid the loan with an interest of Rs. 48,000. Thus the society had to cough up Rs. 1,23,000 to the D.C.C. Bank. This is another live example to show that the LAMPS had failed to develop a good clientele and the members have failed to understand the principle of credit and thereby have taken the public money for granted.

Misappropriation of money has found a place in the affairs of the society. Two sales clerks in the past had misappropriated a sum of Rs. 1,75,000.00. Of this amount, Rs. 52,750 has been recovered from them so far and an amount of Rs. 1,22,250 is still to be recovered. The society is making all efforts including legal action to recover the money.

The society has been formed with 21 objectives and they have been enshrined in its bye-laws which are guiding principles for its governance. But the society has fulfilled only three or four objectives in all these years and it has not bothered to provide services to tribal members by taking up activities as provided in other objectives.

3. LAMPS B.R. HILLS

Biligiri Rangana Hills is situated in Yalandur taluk of the newly created Chamarajanagar district. With a famous temple atop the hill, the place is popularly known as habitat of Soligas, a hill tribe community. The hill is covered by a forest area of 540 square kilometres and is endowed with a large number of minor forest produces and animal species.

LAMPS B.R. Hills was registered on 17.3.1967 as per the Co-operative Societies Act and started functioning about five months later. In the beginning it was called Labour Contract Multi-purpose society. After the introduction of tribal sub-plan it was renamed as large-sized Adivasi Multi-Purpose Co-operative Society. The society has seen many upheavals, with incurring losses in a large number of years.

The area of operation of the society is Yalandur taluka and since the hill tribes people are concentrated in B.R. Hills, the place was chosen to establish LAMPS there. The society has four tribal villages in its area of membership. They are Hosapodu, Purani Podu, Yerakana Gudda and Biligiri Rangana temple.

Membership

The society is known for being situated in a place where only soligas, a hill tribe people are living. All the members of the society belong to that sect of the tribe. The society had a membership of 865 as on 31.3.2002.

Membership and share capital of the society in selected years is shown in the following table.

Table 4.13

Membership and Share Capital in selected years

Sl. No.	*Year*	*No. of Members*	*Share Capital (in Rupees)*
1.	1982-83	216	2,02,160
2.	1987-88	865	4,08,650
3.	1994-95	865	8,39,000
4.	1996-97	865	10,39,000
5.	1998-99	865	14,39,000
6.	2001-02	865	17,48,000

Source: Data personally collected from the society.

Table 4.13 indicates that the membership of the society has remained stagnant at 865 since 1987-88. According to 1991 census Yalandur taluk had a tribal population of 9,036. This is 12.6 per cent of the total population of the taluka of 71,715. Taking into account an average of about 2 per cent increase in population per annum, tribal population stands at around 11,020 in 2002.

Fifty per cent of this population can be considered as potential members. Thus, the society should have had at least 5,000 tribal people as its members. But its membership is less than 18 per cent of potential members. This is really a bad tale. Again, membership is stagnant for the last 13 years.

Share capital of the society has increased from a modest amount of Rs. 2,02,160 in 1982-83 to Rs. 14,39,000 in 1998-99. Of the total share capital of Rs. 14.39 lakhs in 1998-99, share of members amounts to just Rs. 0.70 lakhs and that of Government is Rs. 13.69 lakhs. This shows that the society is heavily dependent upon the government for finances and has failed to mobilise funds from its members.

Objectives

Like other LAMPS in Karnataka State, the LAMPS B.R. Hills has also adopted 21 objectives which are enumerated in its bye-laws. Its main objectives include advancing loans of different types to members, to undertake supplies of food grains and consumer articles to tribal welfare centres and hostels, to take up public works contract in order to provide wage employment to members and to provide assistance to members to build residential houses.

The objectives are wide ranging and if an earnest attempt is made by the society to fulfil these objectives, tribal welfare and transformation of the tribal economy will be really materialised.

Management

The society is managed by a board of directors which consists of 11 members. Six of the directors are elected from among the members and the remaining five are ex-officio directors. They are Assistant Conservator of Forests, Yalandur, Block Development Officer, Tahsildar, nominee of the district Central Co-operative Bank and integrated Tribal Development Programme Officer. Assistant Conservator of Forests who is an ex-officio member is the president of the society. Hence the principle that an elected tribal member should hold the post of President has not been honoured in the society.

The post of the Secretary is held by an Inspector of Co-operative Societies. His services have been lent to the society by the department of co-operation for a certain period. He has been drawing salary and emoluments out of the funds of the society.

Business Activities

LAMPS B.R. Hills has got four retail outlets, one each in four tribal villages or Podus located in its head quarters, that is Biligiri Rangana Hills. Both controlled commodities and non-controlled consumer goods are sold in all the retail outlets. Each retail outlet distributes rationed articles to about 450 card holders. Thus, sale of consumer goods is one of the important activities of the society.

Another important activity of the society is procurement and sale of minor forest produces. It collects MFP from its members and sells them at different outlets. For example, it sells honey at Vivekananda Tribal Welfare Centre at B.R. Hills, and other produces at LAMPS Federation, Mysore and to private traders. Prominent minor forest produces collected by the society are honey, soapnut, treemass, nellikai and tamarind.

Another business of the society is supplying of food grains and consumer articles to tribal welfare centres and hostels in Yalandur taluka.

The society is not engaged in any processing activity and it has no processing unit of its own. It has also not taken up any activity which could impart training to members and help them in pursuit of employment opportunities, such as brick making, basket making etc.,

Thus, the activities of the society are limited to only three i.e., collection and sale of minor forest produces, distribution of rationed goods, sale of consumer articles and supplies of consumer goods to designated institutions.

Table 4.14 indicates total business handled by the society in selected years and profitability. It shows that the society has earned profits in MFP activity in all the selected years. Lease money paid to the forest department and accruals from MFP sales is a pointer to profit margin in that activity. Consumer business and other business have yielded a profit of 7 to 8 per cent on an average.

Financial Assistance by the Government

The society has availed various types of financial assistance from the government in different years. Total amount of loan, share capital and subsidy given by the government to the society are shown in table 4.15.

It amply indicates that the society has availed assistance from the government in the form of share capital, loan and subsidy in a number of years.

Table 4.16 indicates that of the 865 members of the society 74.33 per cent are agricultural labourers. Of the total members 23.34 per cent belonged to the category of marginal farmers owning less than 2 acres of land. Only 20 members or 2.31 per cent of the total members belonged to the category of small farmers. No body owned more than 5 acres of land. Thus, agricultural labourers predominate among the total members of the society.

Table 4.14

Profitability in Business

(Amount in Rupees)

Sl. No.	Year	MFP Sales	Lease Money paid	Sale of Consumer Goods	Purchase of Consumer Goods	Sale of Other Articles	Purchase of Other articles
1	1990-91	1,86,000	12,000	1,32,000	1,21,906	3,12,840	2,80,775
2	1994-95	4,16,000	32,400	3,02,400	2,76,800	4,18,000	3,80,200
3	1996-97	11,32,000	65,600	3,16,000	2,90,416	6,00,000	5,38,918
4	1998-99	6,88,000	1,72,800	3,40,000	3,10,805	5,10,000	4,63,780

Source: Data personally collected from the society.

Table 4.15

Government's Financial Assistance

(Amount in Rupees)

Sl. No.	*Year*	*Share*	*Loan*	*Subsidy*
1.	1966-67	10,000	–	–
2.	1981-82	–	–	25,000
3.	1982-83	25,000	65,000	20,000
4.	1983-84	–	–	65,000
5.	1984-85	50,000	–	–
6.	1985-86	1,20,000	1,15,000	20,000
7.	1986-87	25,000	1,23,000	27,000
8.	1987-88	50,000	35,000	–
9.	1988-89	1,10,000	65,000	–
10.	1990-91	–	63,000	–
11.	1992-93	70,000	–	–
12.	1994-95	1,09,000	–	–
13.	1995-96	3,20,000	–	–
14.	1997-98	4,80,000	–	–
	Total	**13,69,000**	**4,66,000**	**1,57,000**

Source: Data personally collected from the society.

Table 4.16

Membership According to Land Holdings

Sl. No.	*Particulars*	*No. of Members*	*Percentage*
1.	Agricultural Labourers	643	74.33
2.	Less than 1 acre	95	10.98
3.	1 to 2 acres	107	12.36
4.	2 to 5 acres	20	2.31
5.	Above 5 acres	–	–
	Total	**865**	**100.00**

Source: Data personally collected from the society.

Financial Position

Prominent sources of finances of the society are share capital contributed by individual members and the government, reserves and other funds created out of net profit and loans and subsidy by the government. A picture of the financial position of the society as on 31.3.1999 can be seen in the Table 4.17.

Table 4.17

Financial Position as on 31.3.1999

Liabilities	Amount in Rupees	Assets	Amount in Rupees
1. Paid up Share Capital	13,69,160	1. Cash Balance	911
2. Reserve Fund	1,10,402	2. Cash at Bank	2,54,237
3. Loans	5,27,153	Investments	10,66,586
4. Government subsidies	1,57,000	4. Movable and Immovable Assets	2,34,817
5. Other Liabilities	2,12,544	5. Closing stock	3,18,785
6. Audit Objections	3,88,000	6. Medium term loan	29,425
7. Mahadeshwara Traders, Yalandur	19,017	7. MFP Advances and other Recovery	9,72,555
8. Interest on Government Loans	46,666		
9. Suspense Account	12,534		
10. Net profit	35,000		
Total	**28,77,316**	**Total**	**28,77,316**

Source: Data personally collected from the society.

Problems faced by the Society

Problems the society is facing pertain to both its administration and business activity.

Fig. 4.3

Capital Structure of B.R. Hills Lamps 1998-99

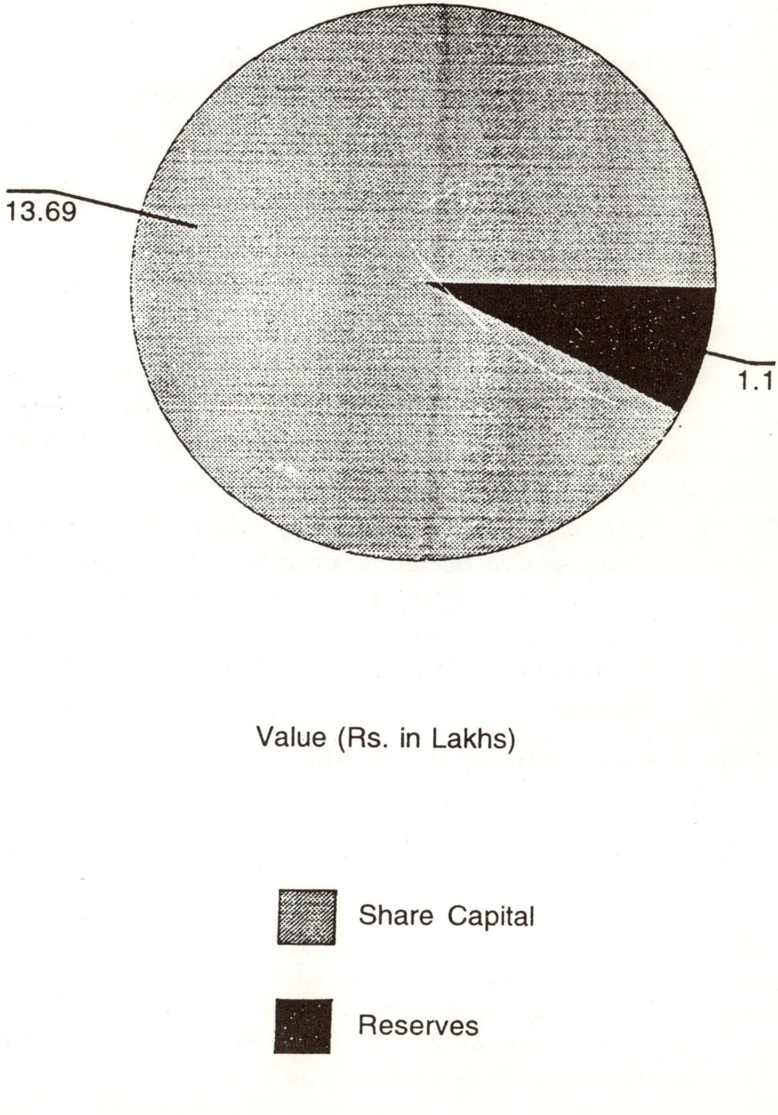

1. There is undue delay in the grant of lease to the society by the forest department. Since the society is prevented from harvesting the produce unless lease is granted, it suffers a loss in its MPF revenues.
2. Lease amount fixed by the state forest department is in excess and unbearable when compared with availability of produce in the designated forest area.
3. Official members of the committee of management do not take keen interest in the development of the society. They do not attend the meetings of the board of directors regularly.
4. Huge amount of funds of the society was misappropriated by ex-employees of the society. Total amount of misappropriation in different years put together is Rs. 4.72 lakhs.
5. The post of the Secretary is held by Inspector of Co-operative Societies, an officer deputed by the government. This arrangement has been there since the beginning. Frequent transfer of Secretary is affecting the functioning of the society.

Critical Assessment of the Working of the Society

An analysis of the working and affairs of the society reveals that it has more failures than successes.

The society has been able to provide employment opportunities to its members. They have been assured of employment for five to six months in the year in the process of harvesting of minor forest produces. Member and adult persons of his family are engaged in the collection and sale of these produces.

Incomes of the tribals have gone up significantly after the organisation of LAMPS. Earlier they were employed by private contractors to collect minor forest produces and were paid very low amount of wages. But the members have been able to get higher returns for the produce they collect and sell to the society. Thus, the society is successful to a great extent in protecting tribals from exploitation.

But the society cannot boast of its achievements as it has missed a lot of avenues and opportunities in transforming the tribal economy.

Membership of the society is stagnant at 865 for more than a decade. Even minimum efforts are not made by the society to enroll new members. This speaks volumes for failure on the part of the society.

A large number of the members are not aware of the nature of functioning of the society, their role in the society and the benefits they can derive from it. The society has miserably failed to create an awareness and spirit of co-operation among its members.

Members of the society are not very much influenced by it. They are under the impression that the society is just an organ of the government.

The society has failed to inculcate the habit of thrift and savings among its members. Enquiries of members during visits to tribal villages have revealed that on an average nearly 80 per cent of the income of the member is frittered away for ccnsumption of alcohol. The tribals in the area are still leading a life of acute poverty. Again, the society has not thought of forming self-help groups of its members to develop the habit of savings among them. The failure of the society is an advantage to Vivekananda Tribal Welfare Centre, a voluntary organisation at B.R.

Hills. The centre has formed 15 self-help groups among tribals and has been arranging awareness camps with the help of its activists.

The society has not paid dividend on the share capital of government and of members.

The society could have garnered a huge amount of profits if it had established a honey processing unit. Instead, the society has been selling honey to Vivekananda Tribal Welfare Centre.

According to Co-operative Societies Act and bye-laws of the society, only an elected tribal director is entitled to hold the post of the president. But that post has been held by Assistant Conservator of Forests. Thus, empowerment of tribals is not thought of even in its minimum sense.

4. LAMPS MUTHATHI

Muthathi, a Pilgrim Centre in Malavalli taluk of Mandya district, borders Kanakapura taluk of Bangalore district. The place is on the banks of Cauvery river and is known to have famous Muthurayaswamy temple.

The society was registered under Karnataka Co-opertive Societies Act on 4.3.1994 and it commenced business in February 1995. It has jurisdiction for the whole of Malavalli taluka. It was the twentieth LAMPS established in Karnataka State and is outside integrated tribal development project area. Taking into account that tribals are concentrated in this place and they have been a neglected lot, it was thought of organising a LAMPS here.

Objectives

Like other LAMPS in Karnataka, the society has got 21 objectives as enshrined in its bye-laws. Its main objectives include providing different types of credit facilities to its members, to supply consumer articles to tribal welfare centres and hostels, to undertake lift irrigation and dairying activities in the name of the society, to develop thrift, self-help and economic discipline among members and to provide financial assistance to members to build residential houses.

Membership

The society has a membership of 300 as on 31.3.2002. The following table depicts its share capital and membership in some selected years.

Table 4.18

Membership and Share Capital in Selected Years

Sl. No.	*Year*	*Number of Members*	*Share Capital (in Rupees)*
1.	1994-95	300	15,000
2.	1995-96	300	15,000
3.	1996-97	300	15,000
4.	1997-98	300	15,000
5.	1998-99	300	15,000
6.	2001-02	300	15,000

Source: Data personally collected from the society.

Membership of the society is stagnant at 300 since its inception. Scheduled tribes population in Malavalli taluka is 1,633 as per the census of 1991. This is 0.61 per cent of total population of 2,64,075 of the whole taluka. Considering a 2 per cent increase in population annually, tribal population of the taluka as in 2002 is 2008. If we take into account that 50 per cent of the population consists of potential members, their number will be 1,004. Thus membership in the society is just 30 per cent of potential members.

The society has a share capital of just Rs. 15,000. Whole of this amount is subscribed by members. In other words, the society has not obtained share capital from the government. As there is no increase in membership, share capital also has remained stagnant.

Management

Board of directors which is the governing body of the society has 11 members in it. Of eleven directors, seven are elected from among tribals and the remaining four are ex-officio. They are Deputy Conservator of Forests. Kanakapura Wildlife Division, Assistant Registrar of Co-operative Societies, Mandya, nominee of the DCC bank and taluka social welfare officer. Deputy Conservator of Forests is the President of the Society.

Business Activities

The society has taken up only one activity i.e., collection and sale of minor forest produce. Only a few items of MFP are collected and sold by the society. They are honey, tamarind and dhoopa. The society has not bothered to take up any other activity like distribution of rationed goods, sale of consumer articles and supplies of food grains to tribal welfare centres as many other LAMPS in Karnataka State have undertaken. It collects minor forest produces from members and sells them to private traders.

Table 4.19

Profitability in Business

(Amount in Rupees)

Year	*MFP Sales*	*Lease Money Paid*
1996-97	1,81,680	30,000
1997-98	4,86,338	40,000
1998-99	26,500	24,000

Source: Data personally collected from the society.

Table 4.19 reveals that the society had paid lease amount of Rs. 94,000 to the state forest department in three years between 1996-97 and 1998-99. Its total earnings from MFP sales in these years have been Rs. 5,94,518. It could not get much profits in 1998-99 as produces were of very low quantity.

Financial Assistance by the Government

The society has availed only subsidy of Rs. 1.00 Lakhs by the State Government in 1995-96 for the purpose of purchase of minor forest produce. The society has not been given loan or share capital by the government.

Membership According to Land Holdings

No member of the society owns land. In other words, all the members are landless persons. They are engaged as MFP collectors and a very few of them are also wage earners under land holders in the nearby places.

Critical evaluation of the working of the Society

Except for the fact that the society has earned a huge amount of profits in a small quantum of business and in a very small period it has been in existence, the performance of the society is really dismal.

The society could have admitted into its fold at least 1,000 potential members in the whole taluka. Instead, it is content with just 300 members, and membership is constant since the beginning. The society has failed to effectively reach out to the people.

Diversification of business is not found place in the society. It is doing only MFP business and has not tried to serve the tribals in as many number of ways as possible.

The State Government had sanctioned Rs. 1.00 Lakh subsidy to the society in 1996-97 for the purchase of forest produce. But the society did not avail it in time and the allocation lapsed at the closure of the financial year 1996-97. This clearly indicates how the authorities of the society have shown negligence in building up the resources.

Table 4.20

Financial position as on 31.3.1999

(Amount in Rupees)

Liabilities	Amount	Assets	Amount
1. Share capital from Members	15,000.00	1. Cash Balance	208.50
2. Deposit of Satyamurthy	8,000.00	2. Current account balance at MDCC bank, Malavalli	4,27,712.00
3. Deposit of Syed Iqbal	3,000.00	3. Current account balance at MDCC bank, Halagur	52,151.00
4. Subsidy from government	1,00,000.00	4. Share capital	15,000.00
5. Deposit	85,000.00	5. Furniture	11,878.00
6. Cash Balance of Secretary	158.75	6. Gunny bags	3,047.00
7. Profit	3,45,399.75	7. Baskets	400.00
		8. Advance from Shivanna	55,200.00
		9. Balance of advance from the President	955.00
		10. Cash balance with the Secretary	7.00
Total	**5,56,558.50**	**Total**	**5,56,558.50**

Source: Data personally collected from the society.

The society has 21 objectives. But it has not ventured to fulfil more than one objective.

Elected tribal person should have been the president of the society as per the provisions of Co-opertive Societies Act and bye-laws of the society. But DCF has occupied the post of President since beginning.

The society does not have a full-time or paid secretary since its inception. Local Range Forest officer acted as Secretary for two years in the beginning, and at present Co-operative development officer, Malavalli, is discharging the duties of Secretary. Absence of a full time secretary is hampering administration and business activities of the society.

5. LAMPS MUDIGERE

LAMPS Mudigere was established on 28.2.1979 ana started functioning about three months later. Mudigere is a taluka head quarters in Chikmagalur district. The place is known for Coffee Plantations as well as lush and ever green forests. The taluka has a large section of working people and tribal populace.

The society has its jurisdiction over three talukas, i.e., Mudigere, Chikmagalur and Kadur. It has enrolled members from 113 tribal colonies of Mudigere taluka, 12 tribal colonies of Chikmagalur taluka and only 1 tribal colony of Kadur taluka. Thus, the activities of the society are much limited to Mudigere taluka and about 88 per cent of its members are only from that taluka.

Membership

The number of tribal families living in the area of operation of the society is 1334. Total tribal population of the three talukas as per 1991 census is 15,555. This is about 2.4 per cent of the total population of these talukas of 6,42,073. The society has a membership of 4,364 as on 31.3.2002.

Table 4.21

Membership and Share Capital in Selected Years

Sl. No.	*Year*	*Number of Members*	*Share Capital (in Rupees)*
1.	1978-79	46	1,00,460
2.	1980-81	1,550	2,15,500
3.	1994-95	3,611	3,42,000
4.	1996-97	4,269	9,80,000
5.	1998-99	4,330	13,95,000
6.	2001-02	4,364	25,18,000

Sources: Data personally collected from the society.

Table 4.21 depicts that the society had a very small membership of 46 in the year of its establishment and it has risen sharply over the years. Total tribal population in the area of its operation as per 1991 census was 15,555. Projection of a two percent increase in population per annum will yield a total tribal population of 18,976 as in 2002. Fifty per cent of this population can be viewed as potential members. In other words, the society could have had a membership of 9,488 by 2002. But its actual membership is only 4,330, which is just 45.5 per cent of its potential members. Thus, the society's performance is very much unsatisfactory on the membership front.

Members of Mudigere LAMPS belong broadly to two tribal sects, i.e. Jenukuruba and Betta Kuruba, the percentage of them in the total membership being roughly about 60 and 40.

The society has a share capital of Rs. 13.95 lakhs as on 31.3.1999. Of this, the share of the government has been Rs. 11.10 lakhs and of members is Rs. 2.85 lakhs.

The percentage of government's share and members' share in the total share capital of the society is 79.6 and 20.4 respectively.

Business Activities

Collection and sale of minor forest produces is one of the major activities undertaken by the society. It is also performing the activities of sale of controlled food articles, cloth, fertilisers, daily requirements and supply of consumer goods to designated institutions like hostels.

The society, in the early years of its inception had a very limited number of activities such as procurement and sale of MFP and distribution of controlled food grains. But, it has been successful in expanding its business. At present it is performing banking activities which have lent credence to its performance. The society collects deposits of different types and advances loans of various types. As on 31.3.1999, it has collected pigmy deposits of Rs. 3.66 lakhs, fixed deposits of Rs. 5.01 lakhs and deposits under LAMPS Savings Certificates to the tune of Rs. 0.16 Lakhs.

The society has been advancing loans out of its funds under different schemes such as pigmy loans, salary scheme loans and jewel loans. Thus, it has found profitable avenues to deploy its funds collected through deposits.

Another important activity being performed by the society is advancing of short-term loans for agricultural purposes and medium term loans for purchase of vehicles, opening of telephone booths etc. Short-term loan is advanced for a period of one year and medium term loan for a period of five years, both at a rate of interest of 14 per cent per annum. As on 31.3.1999 it had advanced short term loans to 98 persons, to the tune of Rs. 10.96 Lakhs and medium term loans to 35 persons to the extent of Rs. 3.70 Lakhs. Percentage of recovery of both these loans is about 90.

The society has set up a soapnut processing unit. It was established in 1985 at a cost of Rs. 1.79 Lakhs. The plant has an installed crushing capacity of 5 quintals per day. But it has been utilised in production only upto 40 per cent of the installed capacity.

Another noteworthy activity undertaken by the society is of imparting training to tribals under different jobs and vocations. Under integrated tribal development programme it has been training interested members to take up tailoring, carpentry and preparation of sericulture implements.

Table 4.22

Profitability in Business

(Amount in Rupees)

Year	*MFP Sales*	*Lease Money paid*	*Purchase of Consumer goods*	*Sale of Consumer goods*
1990-91	–	–	65,49,000	66,00,000
1994-95	27,31,000	2,000	97,24,000	98,00,000
1996-97	34,10,000	11,741	1,61,21,000	1,62,61,000
1998-99	11,40,000	8,960	99,43,200	1,00,34,700

Source: Data personally collected from the society.

Figures in the Table 4.22 indicate that MFP activity is the most profitable one. There is no comparison between the lease amount paid and the earnings from MFP Sales, lease amount being a paltry sum and MFP sales accounting to lakhs of rupees. It can be noticed that the forest department has collected lease amount in different years as token money. Figures in the table show that profit margin in consumer business is to the extent of 8 per cent, which is essential for any business enterprise to sustain itself.

The society has been functioning through ten branches established in different parts of Mudigere taluka.

Management

The society has on its board eleven directors, six elected and the remaining five ex-officio. The ex-officio directors are local Tahsildar, Block Development Officer, Range Forest Officer, Manager of the district central co-operative bank and integrated tribal development plan programme officer. The society has an elected President in a tribal woman.

The society has a paid secretary as its chief executive.

Financial Assistance by the Government

The LAMPS has availed financial assistance from the government to the tune of Rs. 34.99 Lakhs since inception till the end of the financial year of 1999. This includes a share capital of Rs. 11.10 Lakhs, loan of Rs. 9.16 Lakhs and subsidy of Rs. 14.17 Lakhs. Loans availed from the National Co-operative Development Corporation for construction of godowns is also included in this.

Table 4.23

Membership According to Land holdings

Sl. No.	Particulars	No. of Members	Percentage
1.	Agricultural Labourers	3897	90.00
2.	Less than 1 acre	123	2.85
3.	1 to 2 acres	140	3.20
4.	2 to 5 acres	170	3.93
5.	Above 5 acres	–	–
	Total	**4330**	**99.98**

Source: Data personally collected from the society.

Table 4.23 clearly shows that 90 percent of the members are agricultural labourers who are landless. Only

10 per cent of the total members own land. No member possessed more than 5 acres of land.

6.06 per cent of the members own less than 2 acres of land each. Thus about 96.05 per cent of the total members are agricultural labourers and marginal farmers. Among the land holders include 86 coffee growers each of who own between 2 acres and 5 acres of coffee plantations.

Table 4.18 depicts financial position of the society as on 31.3.1999. For the previous years it has a profit of Rs. 1,43,705.

Table 4.24

Financial position as on 31.3.1999

Liabilities	*Amount in Rupees*	*Assets*	*Amount in Rupees*
1. Paid up share capital	13,95,000	1. Cash Balance	55,180
2. Reserves	5,66,129	2. Cash in Banks	1,37,263
3. Loans by Government	9,16,000	3. Investments	2,71,791
4. Subsidies by Government	14,17,000	4. Loans to Members	14,73,455
5. Deposits	8,66,456	5. Movable and Immovable properties	22,17,869
6. Establishment Accounts	1,35,814	6. Advances	57,156
7. Other Liabilities	18,46,056	7. Other assets	1,36,387
8. Profit	1,43,705	8. Credit Bills	14,15,178
		9. Closing stock	15,21,881
Total	**72,86,160**		**72,86,160**

Source: Data personally collected from the society.

Fig. 4.4

Capital Structure of Mudigere Lamps 1998-99

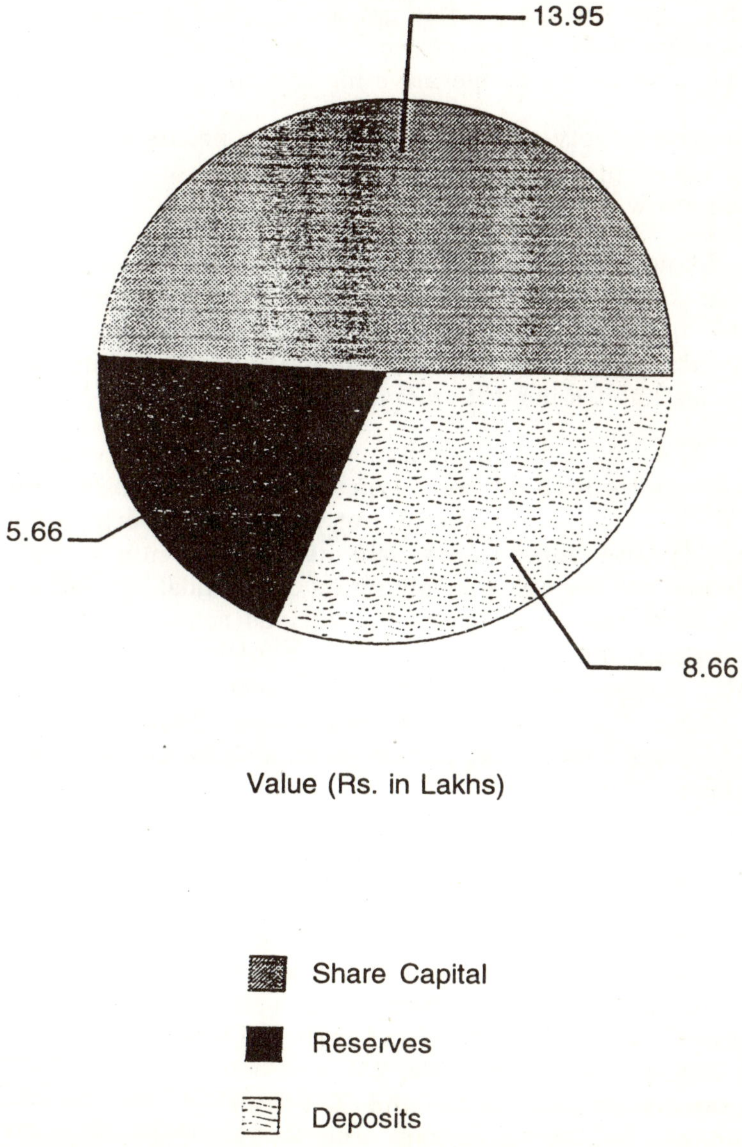

Critical Assessment of the Working of the Society

It was observed by this author during visits to the society and enquiries with the members and the general public that the society has got a very good reputation in Mudigere town and in the whole taluka, and is considered to be a renowned co-operative institution.

The society has been able to earn profits in all the years except two years of 1978-79 when only nominal business was registered and in 1991-92.

A novel feature of Mudigere LAMPS is that like a few other LAMPS in Karnataka State it has undertaken banking activities on the lines of commercial banks. In the way, the society has done its mite to inculcate banking and savings habit among its members and the general public.

The role being played by the society in helping the members through different types of medium-term loans is praiseworthy. It is sanctioning these loans both under subsidy and non-subsidy schemes. Under non-subsidy scheme, the society is involving its own funds. The society has been advancing loans for various schemes such as dairying, small trade, piggery, poultry, purchase of autorickshaws and opening of STD booths. It is a credit to the society that it has sanctioned loans to three handicapped members, each with an amount of Rs. 25,000 to open STD booths.

Thus, the service of the society in employment creation and in income generation is laudable.

The society has created a members' welfare fund. It has undertaken the service of giving away incentives out of this fund to the children of its members who pursue their studies beyond X standard. To encourage their studies, an incentive of Rs. 250 per year to the students pursuing education beyond X Standard, Rs. 500 to students in degree courses and Rs. 1,000 to students pursuing technical, law and medical courses is given. The society has been doing an appreciable service in the field of education.

Even though the society has achieved remarkable progress and is known to have introduced many novel schemes for the benefit of members, its achievement in one important front, i.e., membership is not satisfactory. At the end of the financial year 1998-99 it had a total membership of 4,330, which is by any standards far less when compared with the total tribal population of the area and potential members.

Though the area of operation of the society covers three talukas, its activities are mainly concentrated in and membership is largely from Mudigere taluka. It is found that the society has not evinced much interest in extending its activities to other two talukas, i.e., Chikmagalur and Kadur.

6. LAMPS BASAVANAHALLI

LAMPS Basavanahalli has jurisdiction over entire Somwarpet taluka of Coorg district. Basavanahalli is a village situated at about 30 K.Ms from Somwarpet, on the Mysore-Madikeri road. Since the adjoing places of this village have a large concentration of tribal people, it was found fit to establish LAMPS in this place.

The society was registered on 17.1.1979 and started functioning about five months later. It has jurisdiction over all the tribal colonies of the taluka. The society has got the reputation of being situated in the erstwhile Coorg district the people of which are known for their co-operative character.

Membership

Total membership of the society as on 31.3.2002 has been 2998. Tribal population of Somwarpet taluka as per 1991 census has been 7254 which is 3.97 per cent total population of the taluka. A projection of two per cent increase in population per annum will make the tribal population to be 8,849 in 2002. If half of this is considered as potential members, total membership of the society would have been 4,425. The society's membership consists of both hill tribes and non-hill tribes, their percentage being 25 and 75 respectively.

Amount of share capital of the society as on 33.3.1999 is Rs. 13.07 Lakhs which includes members' share of Rs. 2.07 Lakhs and government's share of Rs. 11.00 Lakhs.

Table 4.25

Membership and Share Capital in Selected Years

Sl. No.	*Year*	*Number of Members*	*Share capital (in Rupees)*
1.	1978-79	271	1,02,710
2.	1984-85	1,149	3,11,490
3.	1990-91	1,671	6,67,000
4.	1994-95	2,890	9,40,000
5.	1996-97	2,988	11,07,000
6.	1998-99	2,988	13,07,000
7.	2001-02	2,998	17,37,000

Source: Data personally collected from the society

Management

Being a taluka level society it has at present 11 directors on the committee of management. Of this 8 directors are elected among the tribal members. Of the remaining three, who are ex-officio directors, one is managing director of the society, another a representative of the financing bank and the other a Range Forest Officer of the area.

The society has on its staff a paid secretary, i.e., chief executive recruited by itself.

Business Activities

The society has undertaken five important activities. They are: (i) Collection and sale of minor forest produces, (ii) consumer business, (iii) supply of foodgrains and consumer articles to tribal welfare centres and hostels, (iv) advancing of term loans, and (v) processing of soapnut. It has opened five retail outlets through which rationed goods and non-controlled articles are sold. These retail outlets are used as branches to collect minor forest produces from members.

The society has been advancing term loans to about 100 members every year for agricultural purposes, poultry, dairying etc. For example, in 1997-98 it had advanced agricultural loans to 15 persons, poultry loans to 80 persons in co-ordination with the scheduled castes and scheduled tribes development corporation and loans to 50 persons to purchase bullock.

The society has set up a soapnut processing unit of its own. It was established in 1993-94 at a cost of Rs. 4.97 Lakhs with an installed crushing capacity of one quintal per hour. Because of bad weather and moisture, soapnut cannot be powdered in the rainy season; and hence the plant is not being utilised to its full capacity.

The society has also taken up the activity of imparting training to members in carpentry and basket making. It has set up a carpentry training unit with the financial assistance of the government.

Figures in table 4.26 clearly indicate that the society has been earning a large amount of profit in MFP business, only exception being in 1994-95 when the lease amount paid was Rs. 60,000 and accruals from MFP sales were Rs. 72,239. This was because in that year a huge quantity of MFP remained unsold and only accruals out of actual

Table 4.26

Profitability in Business

(Amount in Rupees)

Sl. No.	Year	MFP Sales	Lease Money paid	Sale of Consumer Goods	Purchase of Consumer Goods	Sale of Other Articles	Purchase of Other articles
1.	1990-91	2,69,000	57,500	12,38,000	11,51,340	2,01,000	1,82,910
2.	1994-95	72,239	60,000	17,89,000	16,45,879	10,265	9,460
3.	1996-97	5,87,000	70,000	51,10,000	47,52,300	6,23,000	5,54,470
4.	1998-99	5,00,000	1,75,000	40,48,000	37,24,160	5,23,000	4,65,470

Source: Data personally collected from the society.

sales for that particular year are taken into account. Consumer business and supplies to hostels and other designated institutions have yielded a profit margin of 7 to 8 per cent.

Financial Assistance by the Government

The society has availed different types of financial assistance by the government in a number of years since inception. Important types of assistance given to the society have been margin money assistance, additional share capital, subsidy for opening retail outlets, subsidy for procurement of MFP, subsidy for strengthening of share capital base, managerial subsidy and subsidy to set up soapnut processing plant.

The society has so far availed financial assistance to the extent of Rs. 47.15 Lakhs as shown in table 4.27.

Table 4.27

Government's Financial Assistance

(Amount in Rupees)

Sl. No.	*Schemes for which Assistance was availed*	*Amount of loan and share capital*	*Amount of subsidy*
1	Additional	91,000	–
2.	Grants to admit members	–	1,03,500
3.	Loans for Retail outlets	4,57,000	–
4.	Subsidy for Retail outlets	–	90,000
5.	Lease Amount subsidy	–	2,78,000
6.	Share capital subsidy	–	1,04,000
7.	Working capital share	3,00,000	–
8.	Subsidy for training centres	–	4,06,000
9.	Subsidy for Soapnut Processing unit	–	2,00,000
10.	Loan for soapnut processing unit	1,50,000	–

(Table Contd...)

(Table Contd...)

11.	Margin money	–	3,48,000
12.	Loan for Public Distribution	3,000	–
13.	Subsidy for construction of Godown	–	3,10,000
14.	Strengthening of share capital	7,09,000	–
15.	Subsidy for electrification of tribal colonies	–	6,00,000
16.	Subsidy for purchase of Raw Materials	–	2,94,500
17.	Managerial Subsidy	–	71,000
18.	Subsidy for Construction of workshops	–	2,00,000
	Total	**17,10,000**	**30,05,000**

Source: Data personally collected from the society.

Table 4.28

Membership according to land holdings

Sl. No.	*Particulars*	*No. of Members*	*Percentage*
1.	Agricultural labourers	2,020	67.60
2.	Less than 1 acre	515	17.23
3.	1 to 2 acres	348	11.65
4.	2 to 5 acres	87	2.91
5.	Above 5 acres	18	0.60
	Total	**2,988**	**99.99**

Source: Data personally collected from the society.

Table 4.28 amply reveals that agricultural labourers predominate in the membership of the society. They constitute 67.60 per cent of the total members. More than 96 per cent of the members belong to the category of agricultural labourers and marginal farmers. Small farmers constitute just 2.91 per cent. Only 18 persons or 0.60 per cent of total members own above five acres of land.

The society has earned a net profit of Rs. 1,59,438 as on 31.3.1999. Its financial statement reveals that closing stock and movable and immovable properties are also of very high value.

Table 4.29

Financial position as on 31.3.1999

	Liabilities	*Amount*		*Assets*	*Amount*
1.	Paid-up share capital	13,07,000	1.	Closing cash balance	21,739
2.	Welfare fund	19,404	2.	Cash balance at Bank	11,65,110
3.	Other Funds	6,02,743	3.	Investments	6,63,291
4.	Deposits	1,44,431	4.	Immovable and movable properties	32,95,120
5.	Loans from Government	6,10,000	5.	Loans to Members	1,08,942
6.	Subsidy by Government	30,05,000	6.	Adjustment Accounts	2,58,515
7.	Adjustment loans	28,738	7.	Stock shortage to be recovered	1,72,597
8.	Reserves	1,87,762	8.	Closing Stock	4,20,987
9.	For interest payment on government loans	31,785			
10.	Net profit	1,59,438			
	Total	**60,96,301**		**Total**	**60,96,301**

Source: Data personally collected from the society.

Problems faced by the Society

During visits to the society and after enquiries with the secretary and some of the members of the committee of management the following problems were noticed.

Fig. 4.5
Capital Structure of Basavanahalli Lamps
1998-99

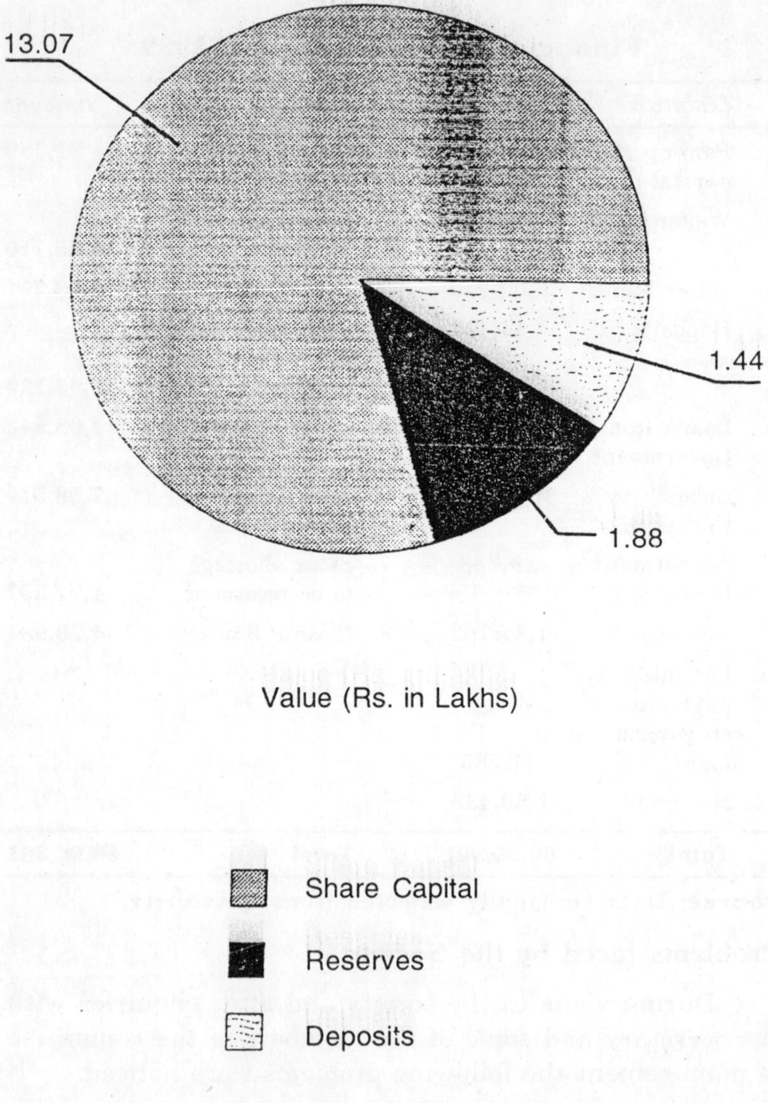

1. There has been undue delay in the grant of lease to the society by the forest department. The society is forced to lose a lot of revenue as it cannot harvest MFP when the earlier lease is expired and the new lease is not granted.
2. Unauthorised collection of MFP by non-tribals and private contractors has been there on a large scale.
3. Funds of the society have been misappropriated to the extent of Rs. 2,26,797 by five ex-employees of it. The society has not yet been able to recover the money involved in misappropriation.

Critical Assessment of the Working of the Society

By and large the performance of the society is good. It has got reputation of being one of the viable LAMPS in Karnataka State.

The society has fared badly in the field of enrolment of members. Total tribal population of Somwarpet taluk as per 1991 census was 7,254. A two per cent increase in population per annum can be projected and that takes us to 8,849 tribal population as in 2002. Fifty per cent of this could be considered as potential members, i.e., who could have been actually admitted and that will be 4,425. But total membership in the society in 2002 has been 2998 which is less than the number of potential members to the extent of about 18 per cent.

The society has shown its mettle in availing a very huge amount of subsidy under a number of schemes and it has made use of this facility effectively.

But the dark side of the picture is that the society has utterly failed to embrace other activities such as banking, which could have helped both the society and the members. It is to be admitted that the society is situated just five K. Ms. away from Kushalnagar, a big town and hence it cannot be in a position to attract deposits from the general public and may also not be able to fruitfully deploy its funds in the form of loans. But it could have ventured to introduce banking services at least in a small measure to inculcate savings habits among members, as also formation of self help groups to promote thrift and self-help among its economically poor members.

7. LAMPS UDUPI

LAMPS Udupi was established on 23.2.1977 and commenced functioning about fifteen days later. The society is located at Adi Udupi, an important and age old extension in Udupi city.

Udupi is one of a few coastal districts of Karnataka State. Udupi district was carved out of the erstwhile South Kanara district, also called Mangalore district, in 1998. Before it became a separate district, it was one of the talukas of South Kanara district. Udupi is a prominent religious city and an important commercial centre.

LAMPS Udupi has jurisdiction over all the 115 revenue villages of the taluka. It had earned profits in all the years since its establishment.

Membership

The society had a total membership of 6,002 as on 31.3.2002.

The following table 4.30 indicates membership and share capital of the society in some select years.

It can be seen from the above table that membership in the society has increased from 3401 in 1990-91 to 6,002 in 2001-02 its share capital has gone up from Rs. 2,34,010 to Rs. 37,33,000 in the same period.

Table 4.30

Membership and Share Capital in Selected Years

Sl. No.	*Year*	*Number of Members*	*Share Capital (in Rupees)*
1.	1990-91	3,405	2,34,010
2.	1994-95	4,349	4,91,277
3.	1995-96	4,803	7,35,907
4.	1996-97	4,867	13,74,538
5.	1997-98	4,965	17,10,557
6.	1998-99	5,459	22,62,000
7.	2001-02	6,002	37,33,000

Source: Data personally collected from the society.

Total scheduled tribes population of Udupi taluka as per 1991 census has been 20,381. This is 4.11 per cent of the total population of the taluka of 4,95,766. A projection of two per cent increase in population per annum will yield total tribal population of 24,869 in 2002. If 50 per cent of this number can be considered potential members, the latter would have been 12,435. But actual membership in the society is 6,002 which is 48 per cent of potential members. There has been a consistent increase in the membership of the society.

The society had share capital of the amount of Rs. 22.62 Lakhs as on 31.3.1999. Of this, share of members is Rs. 2.29 Lakhs and of government is Rs. 20.33 Lakhs. Of the total share capital, the percentage of members' share and government's share is 10.1 and 89.9 respectively.

Management

Being a taluka level society LAMPS, Udupi has eleven directors in its committee of management. Of this, nine directors are elected from among members and the remaining two are ex-officio directors. These two are: (i) managing director of the society and (ii) integrated tribal development project co-ordinator. The committee is headed by the President who is an elected director.

The Chief Executive of the society is designated as 'Managing Director' who is an officer of the co-operation department and whose services are hired from the government.

Business Activities

The activities undertaken by LAMPS, Udupi provide an interesting picture. Its main activities are: (i) collection and sale of minor forest produces, (ii) distribution of rationed goods, (iii) sale of cloth and daily requirement, (iv) supplies of food grains and other consumer articles to hostels and other designated institutions and (v) banking. It has got a carpentry unit which is used as training-cum-production centre. The society has rented out a part of its building to house a centre for training candidates in gem cutting. This also is used as a training-cum-production centre. Thus, the society has taken up both credit and non-credit activities.

The society has no earmarked forest area for collection of M.F.P. Instead, it has been permitted by the forest department to collect dhoopa, a minor forest produce, from road-side trees. Thus, the society has been collecting and selling only dhoopa.

One of the important activities taken up by the society is advancing of short-term, medium-term and long-term loans to its members. It has been advancing these term loans since 1994-95 for seasonal agricultural operations, purchase of cattle, digging of wells and land development. In 1998-99 total amount of term loans advanced was

Rs. 26.24 Lakhs. Of this, short-term loan was of the order of Rs. 4.97 Lakhs, medium-term loan was to the extent of Rs. 14.19 Lakhs and long-term loan was of the order of Rs. 7.08 Lakhs.

Recovery of loans advanced under these schemes has been to the extent of 100 percent.

The society has set up a carpentry training-cum-production centre at Hanumanthanagar of Puttur village.

LAMPS Udupi has opened two retail outlets, one at Barkur and the other at Athradi. Consumer goods, rationed goods and cloth are sold at these outlets.

Banking is another important activity undertaken by the Society. This activity is being done as in any commercial bank or co-operative bank. The society is engaged in collection of deposits under various schemes such as savings bank account, recurring deposit, pigmy account and fixed deposit. It has introduced 'Giri Nidhi Cash Certificates' to mobilise deposits for a fixed term.

The society has been advancing loans on deposits, jewel loans and loans to salaried persons. In 1998-99, total loans advanced by the society under these schemes was of the order of Rs. 4. 60 Lakhs.

Recovery of loans under these schemes is also to the extent of 100 percent.

Banking activity undertaken by the society has proved to be very profitable and service oriented. It mobilises term deposits at different rates of interest and advances loans at such rate of interest as to obtain three to six percent of profit depending upon the period of loan. For example, the society pays interest of 14 percent per annum on fixed deposits accepted for more than one year, six percent on savings deposits, twelve percent per annum on recurring deposits and one percent on pigmy deposits. The Giri Nidhi Certificate floated by it will double in value in a period of five years.

As part of banking activity, the society is doing the service of discounting cheques given to beneficiaries given by municipality and government offices. In this way it helps people to collect money in lieu of cheques without loss of time. Commission charged for discounting of cheques is Rs. 6 per Rs. 1,000. The society has been earning on an average Rs. 1,200 per day in this activity.

Table 4.31

Profitability in Business

Year	*MFP Sales*	*Lease Money Paid*	*Sale of Consumer Goods*	*Purchaseof Consumer Goods*
1990-91	14,28,000	2,05,483	12,16,733	11,30,406
1992-93	–	–	27,57,340	25,54,315
1994-95	–	–	22,52,000	20,95,300
1996-97	6,10,000	1,08,000	16,15,000	14,86,650
1998-99	2,88,000	61,500	17,50,000	16,27,500

Source: Data Personally collected from the society.

Figures in table 4.31 indicate that both MFP activity and consumer business of the society have yielded profits in all the select years. Sale of consumer goods, which also includes distribution of rationed articles, has yielded a profit of around seven percent on an average in all the years of MFP activity.

Financial Assistance by the Government

The society has availed various types of financial assistance from the government. The following table shows the financial assistance of different types availed by the society under various schemes.

Table 4.32

Government's Financial Assistance

Sl. No.	*Schemes for which Assistance was availed*	*Amount of share capital*	*Amount of Loan*	*Amount of Subsidy*
1.	Construction of Godown	–	3,95,00	50,875
2.	Establishment Expenditure	–	–	50,000
3.	Membership of Grants	–	–	59,125
4.	Share capital	15,92,000	–	–
5.	Additional Share capital	25,000	–	–
6.	Margin money	1,41,000	–	–
7.	Opening of Retail Outlets	–	80,000	20,000
8.	Fuel Depot	–	35,000	15,000
9.	Additional Share capital	2,75,000	–	–
	Total	**20,33,000**	**5,10,000**	**1,95,000**

Source: Data personally collected from the society.

Table 4.33

Membership According to Land Holdings

Sl. No.	*Particulars*	*No. of Members*	*Percentage*
1.	Agricultural Labourers	4,027	73.8
2.	Less than 1 acre	240	4.4
3.	1 to 2 acres	512	9.4
4.	2 to 5 acres	680	12.4
5.	Above 5 acres		
	Total	**5459**	**100.0**

Source: Data personally collected from the society.

The above table indicates that 73.8 percent of the members of the society are landless agricultural labourers. Only 26.2 percent of the total members own land. 13.8 percent of members own less than 2 acres of land each. Thus, about 87.6 percent of members are agricultural labourers and marginal farmers. Small farmers, i.e, with 2 to 5 acres each, account for 12.4 percent of the total members. No member owns more than 5 acres.

An interesting feature is that of the 1,432 members who own land, about 800 members, i.e., 55.8 percent of total land holder members, are in possession of land owing to land reforms and the progressive policy of tiller is the owner of the soil.

Table 4.34

Financial Position as on 31.3. 1999

	Liabilities	*Amount in Rupees*		*Assets*	*Amount In Rupees*
1.	Paid up share capital	22,62,000	1.	Cash balance	1,85,287
2	Deposits	27,93,503	2.	Bank Accounts	10,41,480
3.	Security Deposit	1,79,805	3.	Investments	8,20,874
4	Reserves	13,42,138	4.	Share Certificates	59,311
5	Subsidy by the Government	1,95,000	5.	Loans to Members	29,96,360
6	Subsidy to members	1,10,613	6	Credit Bills	6,01,647
7	Depreciation Fund	Immovable 6,40,395	7.	Movable and Immovable properties	20,07,034
8	Miscellaneous Liabilities	1,05,612	8	Closing Stock	1,69,465
9	Undistributed Profit	97,592			
10	Profit for 1998-99	1,53,800			
	Total	**78,80,458**		**Total**	**78,80,458**

Source: Data personally collected from the society.

Fig. 4.6

Capital Structure of Udupi Lamps 1998-99

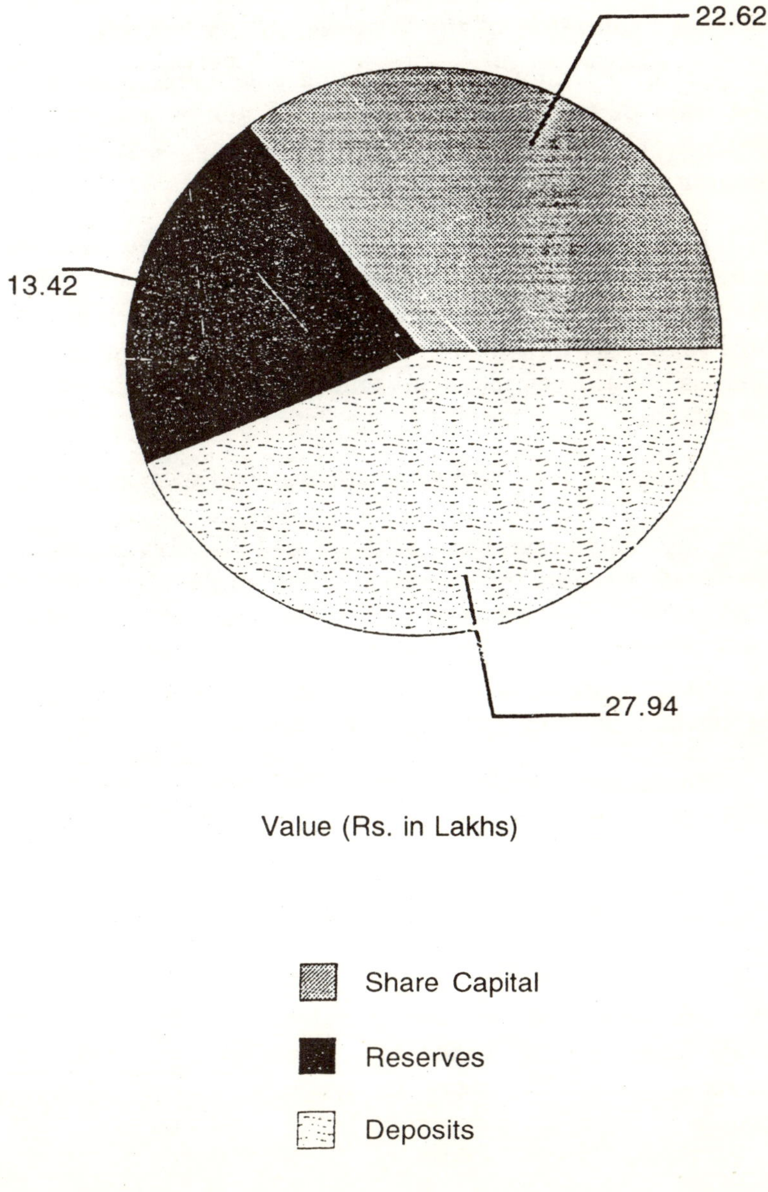

Table 4.34 depicts financial position of the society as on 31.3.1999. It had earned a profit of Rs. 1,53,800 for the year 1998-99.

Critical Evaluation of the Working of the Society

LAMPS Udupi has been doing a laudable service in the field of tribal development. Its achievements are praiseworthy in MFP business, banking activity and lending of term loans.

Eventhough no forest area is earmarked for the society, it has been able to collect minor forest produce from the roadside trees. It has shown its worth by churning out MFP business amounting to lakhs of rupees and in the process creating employment and income earning avenues for tribals.

Its banking activities are unparalleled with any other LAMPS in Karnataka. It has developed this activity on par with any commercial bank or developed co-operative bank. Cheques discounting service it has undertaken is an indicator of society's thinking on the lines of developing good clientele and diversification of activities. Its contribution in developing banking habit among people, particularly among tribals, is remarkable.

Short term, medium-term and long-term loans being advanced by the society have proved to be of great help to tribal farmers. There is heavy demand for these loans from members. The society has plans to distribute a minimum of Rs. 100 Lakhs of term loans to members in the year 1999-2000.

The society has adopted a method of giving incentive to its directors with a view to improve their participation in its activities. Directors' involvement in enrolling new members, their attendance in board meetings and their participation in business activities are judged to declare incentive. Five percent of the net profit to be appropriated is earmarked for this purpose.

On the face of it, any one can easily think that the society is not doing a remarkable job and it is replica of a commercial bank as it is very much involved in lending term loans and in discharging banking activities. One can assume that members and non-members could have obtained these facilities in any commercial or co-operative bank. But the efforts of the society in organising the tribals and attracting them to get different facilities under one roof has been a marvellous job.

The society has an important grouse in that though it is shown that it has been earning a profit of 8 to 9 percent in 'other business' i.e., in supplies of goods to hostels and other designated institutions, actual profit margin will not be that much. This is because there is inordinate delay in making payments for these supplies by the concerned authorities. It usually takes four to six months for the society to get payment. The society is forced to pay interest on the funds borrowed to make the supplies of goods. This is causing a heavy financial burden on the society.

8. LAMPS HEGGADADEVANANKOTE

Heggadadevanakote is one of the most backward talukas in the State of Karnataka. It is in Mysore district and impockets a large chunck of tribal population.

LAMPS Heggadadevanakote was registered on 30.12.1976 and commenced its business about a month later. The society is situated at Heggadadevanakote proper. It found its existence in 1965 when it was registered as Tribal Labour Co-operative Society. Its earlier registration was cancelled and was re-registered as Large-sized Adivasi Multi-purpose Co-operative Society in 1976 as part of tribal sub-plan strategy. The jurisdiction of the society is the whole of Heggadadevanakote taluka and it had membership of 4,475 at the end of March 2002.

Membership

Members of the society belong to both hill tribes and non-hill tribes, their percentage among total members being around 90 and 10 respectively. The important tribes which have their representatives in membership are soligas, betta Kuruba, Jenu Kuruba, Yeravas and Panias.

Total tribal population of Heggadadevanakote Taluka as per 1991 census was 11,321. This is 5.2 percent of the total population of the taluka of 2,16,399. Projection of a 2 percent growth in population will yield total tribal population of 13,807 in 2002.

Table 4.35

Membership and Share Capital in Selected Years

Sl. No.	*Year*	*Number of Members*	*Share Capital (in Rupees)*
1.	1990-91	2,150	1,21,500
2.	1992-93	3,120	3,16,600
3.	1994-95	3,370	4,14,596
4.	1996-97	4,205	7,91,056
5.	1998-99	4,456	8,18,193
6.	2001-02	4,475	11,10,000

Source: Data personally collected from the society.

Number of members in the society has gone up from 2,950 in 1990-91 to 4,456 in 1998-99 and to 4,475 in 2002. It shows that there has been a consistent increase in membership.

The society has total share capital of Rs. 8.18 Lakhs as on 31.3.1999. Of this, share of members is Rs. 0.95 Lakhs and of government is Rs. 7.23 Lakhs. Of the total share capital, the percentage of members' share and government's share has been 11.6 and 88.4 respectively. As the table reveals the amount of share capital has gone up from Rs. 2,10,100 in 1990-91 to Rs. 8,18,193 in 1998-99.

Management

LAMPS Heggadadevanakote has eleven directors in its committee of management. Of this, six directors are elected from among members and the remaining five are ex-officio directors. They are: (i) Range Forest Officer, (ii) Block Development Officer, (iii) Tahasildar, (iv) Integrated Tribal Development Project Co-ordinator and (v) Manager of the local branch of the Mysore district central co-operative bank. The committee is headed by the President who is an elected director.

The Chief Executive of the society is designated as 'Secretary' and is a paid employee, i.e., a person recruited by the society itself.

Business Activities

The activities of the society are just traditional in the sense that it has so far undertaken only the activities of collection and sale of MFP, distribution of rationed goods and supplies of food grains and the consumer articles to designated institutions and advancing term loans. In other words, the society has taken up both credit and non-credit activities. It has given loans in many years under government-sponsored schemes involving loanable funds of the district central co-operative bank and subsidy doled out by the government. These schemes are mainly integrated rural development programme and sericulture development.

The society had advanced term loans only in a few years on the whole to 177 members. Of this, short-term loan has been advanced to 28 members involving Rs. 76,000 and medium term loans to 149 members involving Rs. 9.00 Lakhs. Recovery of these loans has been to the extent of about 40 percent.

The society has opened two retail outlets. In one of these outlets both rationed goods and non-controlled consumer goods are sold and in another outlet only rationed goods are sold.

Some years ago, the Society has taken up the activities of basket making and brick making. These activities were given up for lack of professionalisation.

Minor forest produces business is really the main activity of this society. But of late, the extent of forest area leased to it has dwindled and these are prominently scrub forests covered by deciduous trees and bushes. Two ranges of local forest area, i.e., Heggadadevanakote range and Sargur range are leased out to the society for MFP procurement.

Table 4.36 amply indicates that the society has not been able to obtain much profit out of MFP activity in 1990-91 and 1994-95. But profitability in this activity in 1996-97 and 1998-99 has been good.

Profitability in consumer business, is of the order of seven to eight percent on an average in the selected years.

Financial Assistance by the Government

Government has provided different types of financial assistance to the society. These include loans, share capital and subsidy.

Table 4.36
Profitability in Business

Year	MFP Sales	Lease Money Paid	Sale of Consumer Goods	Purchase of Consumer Goods
1990-91	2,78,000	1,17,500	1,86,000	1,71,800
1992-93	–	–	2,31,000	2,13,415
1994-95	1,28,000	82,500	2,46,000	2,28,000
1996-97	8,80,000	2,66,000	2,65,000	2,42,100
1998-99	10,98,000	2,70,000	2,00,000	1,86,500

Source: Data personally collected from the society.

Table 4.38 shows that 2,526 members or 56.7 per cent of total members of the society are landless. Marginal farmers account for 25.7 per cent of total members. Only 13.6 per cent of total members i.e., 605 members own between 2 and 5 acres each. No member owns more than 5 acres of land.

Table 4.37
Government's Financial Assiatance

Sl. No.	Schemes for which Assistance was availed	Amount of loan and share capital (in Rupees)	Amount of Subsidy (in Rupees)
1.	Working capital share	7,23,000	–
2.	Loan for retail outlet	1,20,000	–
3.	Subsidy for retail outlet	–	30,000
4.	Margin money	–	50,000
5.	Loan for Fuel Depot	35,000	–
6.	Subsidy for fuel depot	–	15,000
7.	Additional share loan	75,000	–
8.	Working capital loan	5,60,000	–
9.	Loan for godown construction	1,30,000	–
10.	Lease amount subsidy	–	2,30,000
11.	Interest free loan for business activity	1,55,000	–
12.	Subsidy for processing unit	–	1,40,000
	Total	**17,98,000**	**4,65,000**

Source: Data personally collected from the society.

Table 4.38

Membership According to Land Holdings

Sl. No.	Particulars	No. of Members	Percentage
1.	Agricultural Labourers	2,526	56.7
2.	Less than 1 acre	470	10.5
3.	1 to 2 acres	855	19.2
4.	2 to 5 acres	605	13.6
5.	Above 5 acres	–	–
	Total	**4,456**	**100.0**

Source: Data personally collected from the society.

Table 4.39

Financial Position as on 31.3.1999

Liabilities	Amount in Rupees	Assets	Amount in Rupees
1. Paid up share capital	8,18,193	1. Cash Balance	8,697
2. Reserve Fund	35,394	2. Bank Accounts	3,45,354
3. Other Funds	79,909	3. Investments	1,07,360
4. Loans for DCC Bank	3,36,553	4. Movable and Immovable properties	29,853
5. Loans from Government	1,07,597	5. Advances to be recovered	4,92,265 4,92,265
6. Subsidy from Government	2,00,000	6. Loans from Members	88,259
7. Deposits	74,506	7. Value of closing stock	1,14,430
8. Other Liabilities	22,497	8. Other Assets	2,69,431
		9. Net Loss	2,19,000
Total	**16,74,649**		**16,74,469**

Source: Data personally collected from the society.

Fig. 4.7

Capital Structure of Heggada Devanakote Lamps 1998-99

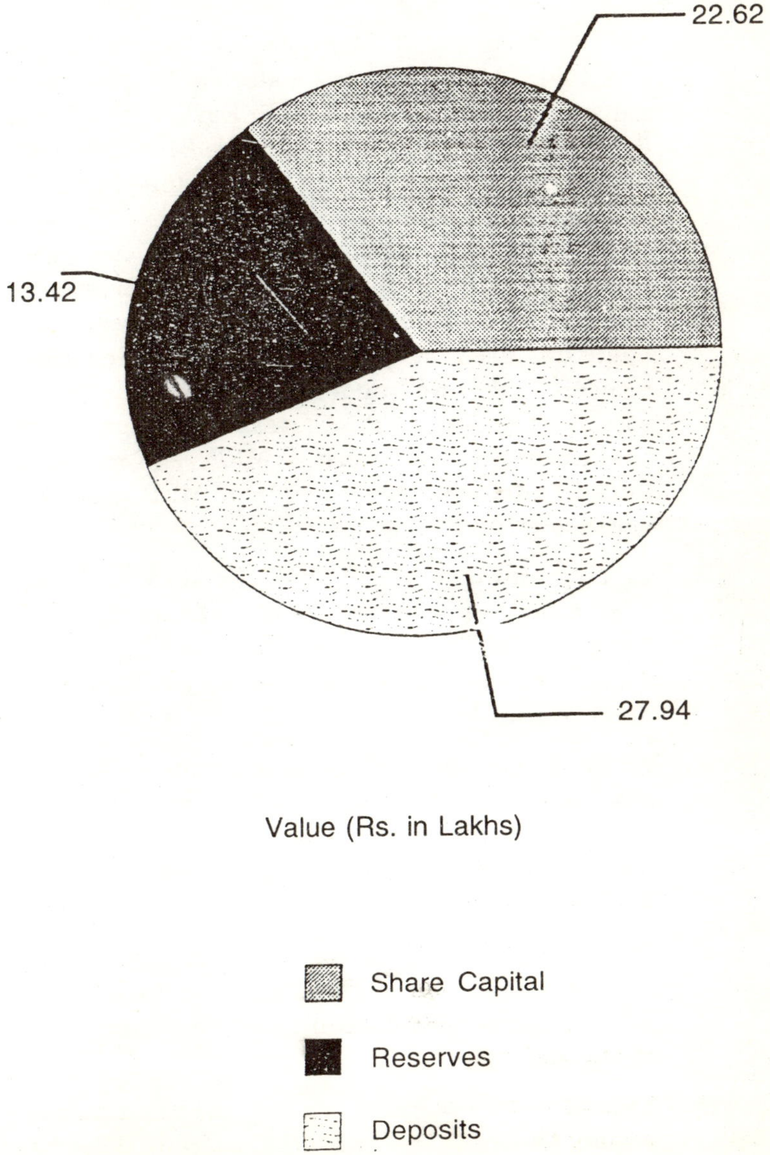

Problems Faced by the Society

The following are the important problems being faced by the society

1. MFP business of the society is not much profitable. Lease amount collected by the forest department is unusually high. Earlier, the forest department used to lease out land hectare-wise. At present, the system has been changed and the area is being leased out range-wise. This is disadvantageous to the society because, area wise the ranges may be small. Much of the forest area which was earlier being leased to the society has been declared as protected area under tiger project. Only two ranges are leased out to the society at present. These forests with scrubs and bushes do not bear much of MFP. The society is forced to forego huge amount of MFP resources because of this.

2. Lease amount fixed by the state forest department is in excess and unbearable when compared with the availability of produce in the designated forest area. Lease money is fixed most unscientifically.

3. There is inordinate delay in the grant of lease to the society by the forest department. As the society is not expected to harvest the produce till the lease is granted, it suffers a great deal in its MFP revenues.

4. Official members of the committee of management do not attend board meetings regularly. They have failed to take keen interest in the activities of the society.

5. Tribals in this segment are very poor and literacy among them is just around 15 per cent. They are

really at a loss to have a knowledge of the activities of the society and the importance of their participation in its activities. This is one of the main reasons for stunted growth and poor performance of the society.

Assessment of the Working of the Society

LAMPS Heggadadevanakote has more failures than successes on its part. It is still performing under heavy accumulated losses.

Failure of the society in the membership front is conspicuous. Total tribal population of Heggadadevanakote taluka in 2002 has been about 13,807. Half of this can be considered as number of potential members. Thus the number of potential members is 6,900, which the society could have enrolled. But actual membership in the society is just 4,475 in 2002 which is 65 per cent of potential members.

The society has failed to take up new activities and to diversify business. It could have introduced many a training-cum-production scheme which are of great help to tribal people.

Main Findings in the Chapter

Important findings in this chapter have corroborated and are in conformity with our findings in the third chapter.

Actual membership in the LAMPS is far less than the potential members. Except Udupi LAMPS, other societies have not made much of an effort to enrol a large number of potential members in the area of their operation.

Contrary to the Co-operative Societies Act, four societies of B.R. Hills, Chamarajanagar, Hunsur and

Muthathi have forest officers as their Presidents. They have failed to make an elected director as the President of the Society.

Four societies, that is of Heggadadevanakote, Basavanahalli, Mudigere and Hunsur have paid secretaries as their Chief Executives. Udupi, B.R. Hills and Chamarajanagar LAMPS have full time secretaries, who are officers of the co-operation department and who are deputed by the government. Only Muthathi LAMPS has an in-charge secretary who is an officer of the co-operation department.

Among the LAMPS selected for case studies, only Chamarajanagara LAMPS has an accumulated profit of Rs. 23.92 Lakhs. The other five LAMPS have a very small amount of accumulated profits. Enquiries have revealed that except for LAMPS Udupi, other four societies had a very large amount of accumulated losses in many years and they have concentrated their efforts to wipe out these losses. LAMPS of Hunsur and Heggadadevanakote have incurred heavy amount of accumulated losses. It is a pity that inspite of hefty sums of money pumped in by the government to these societies in the forms of share capital, loan and subsidy, these societies are prone to incur losses. Lack of awareness to handle different types of business, misappropriation of funds in some societies, decline in MFP revenues are some of the important reasons for heavy losses. Inordinate delay on the part of government agencies to make payment for the supplies made by LAMPS is also one of the reasons for losses.

Only two LAMPS, that is of Udupi and Chamarajanagar have earned profits in all the years since their establishment.

There has been undue delay in the grant of lease by the forest department. LAMPS are not permitted to harvest

MFP till the lease is granted. This has forced these societies to forego much of MFP revenues.

Advances and recoveries are an important item of assets involving huge amounts in Chamarajanagar and B.R. Hills LAMPS. These are the advance payments made to MFP collectors and agents before the produce is delivered by them. In many years, these agents and collectors have made short deliveries and hence money is to be recovered from them.

Except for LAMPS Heggadadevanakote, borrowings in other societies are either nil or negligible. Only Heggadadevanakote LAMPS has borrowings to the tune of Rs. 3.36 Lakhs as on 31.3.1999.

It was pointed out in the beginning of this chapter that people of Coorg and South Kanara districts are supposed to possess a strong co-operative character. This is proved in the case of LAMPS Udupi of erstwhile South Kanara District. The society has made notable strides in enrolment of members and business expansion. It has developed a very good network of loaning and deposit mobilisation and its lending operations are truly co-operative in character. Recovery of loans is almost 100 per cent which proves that needy people take recourse to borrowing and make prompt repayments. Eventhough the society has no forest area earmarked for it, it has been successful in collecting MFP from roadside trees. Its members are largely involved in this business and as a result they have been able to get employment and to increase their incomes. But the same is not fully true in the case of LAMPS Basavanahalli of Coorg district. The society, no doubt, has involved a large number of tribals in collection of MFP and thereby it has succeeded in improving their economic conditions. But it has failed to evolve lending and deposit mobilisation operations because of which members and tribal non-members are deprived of the opportunity of developing savings habits and to avail loan facilities. Hence, the co-operative character of members of this LAMPS has not been put to test.

Assets and Liabilities items of LAMPS Muthathi are a few. The society has not developed a proper structure of reserves and deposits. The main reasons for this is that the society has not ventured to diversify its business and to enlarge its membership.

CHAPTER — 5

A Model for Lamps

In the previous chapter, a study of eight selected LAMPS in their broader aspects had been undertaken. Performance of these LAMPS provides a mixed picture in that only some LAMPS have been partially successful in their objectives, their performance varies from one LAMPS to the other and even within the LAMPS, the performance of some societies is dismal. An overview of the performance of LAMPS in India had been undertaken in the II Chapter and a study of performance of LAMPS in Karnataka and case studies of selected LAMPS in Karnataka have been done in III and IV Chapters respectively. Based on the observations made in these chapters and based on the view gathered by this author about the functioning as well as reasons for success and failures of LAMPS, a model for the working of LAMPS has been suggested in the present chapter.

Since LAMPS are co-operative institutions comparatively of recent origin, they have been organised to accomplish welfare exclusively of one section of the society, i.e., scheduled tribes, and since there is an element of imposition rather than voluntarism in the formation of these societies, it has been found essential to suggest a model for their successful working. Again, the pattern of these societies in terms of their organisation, administration and business activity differs from state to state as also within the state. During visits to LAMPS and enquiries with stake holders this author has found that people in many LAMPS in Karnataka are not actually aware of the activities these societies have to undertake and the real nature of their functioning.

It is in the background of these factors, an earnest attempt is made in this chapter to evolve a suitable model for the working of LAMPS in India.

While suggesting such a model for LAMPS, note has to be taken regarding the factors which affect their working. Such a model should stretch out to organisational, administrative, business and other aspects of LAMPS. Based on successes and failures in the working of LAMPS and relevant causes thereto, the model should be able to provide a frame work which can act as a guide to proper working of these societies.

Organisation

Organisational pattern of LAMPS in India does not exhibit a similarity, it differs from state to state and even within the state. The study team on co-operative structure in tribal development project areas, popularly known as Bawa Committee, had recommended that LAMPS should be established with one tehsil or block as its area of operation. This can at best be adjudged as the ideal pattern for formation of LAMPS. But in the regions where tribal population and number of potential members are large and membership is unwieldy, to serve the members effectively, it can be suggested that more than one LAMPS have to be organised in a tehsil or block.

To take a few examples, in Maharashtra there are four to five LAMPS in each tehsil, in Tamil Nadu, each LAMPS has jurisdiction over one tehsil, in Orissa, the pattern is mixed with 46 LAMPS covering a block each in its area of operation, whereas the rest of the LAMPS have been organised at the rate of two or three LAMPS per block, in Karnataka, 18 LAMPS covering a tehsil in their area of operation, one LAMPS covering two tehsils and two LAMPS having three tehsils in their area of operation and in Bihar and Madhya Pradesh each tehsil having about three to four LAMPS.

Co-operatives in India have a definite structure, each type of co-operatives having a certain jurisdiction. For example, taluka agricultural produce co-operative marketing societies have been organised at the rate of one per each taluka, each primary co-operative agricultural and rural development bank also called land development bank covers one taluka in its area of operation, primary credit society extends its area of operation over just a few villages, milk producers' co-operative societies have jurisdiction over a few villages, federations of primary credit societies, i.e., district central co-operative banks have been organised at the rate of one per each district so on and so forth. In the same way, LAMPS can have also a definite structure and a definite area of operation. It can be suggested that each LAMPS should have one tehsil or block as its area of operation.

Each LAMPS, in its area of operation, can have as many number of branches or outlets as necessary based upon the volume of business, number of members and the extent of the area of operation.

The second aspect that has be to considered with regard to organisation of LAMPS is membership. In a large number of states in India, persons belonging to scheduled castes are also being enrolled as members of LAMPS. But in the state of Karnataka and the union territory of Daman and Diu only scheduled tribes persons are admitted as members of LAMPS. These societies have been organised in India as part of tribal sub-plan and with a view to cater to all the needs of tribals under one single roof. Thus, it is of utmost importance *that membership in LAMPS should be restricted only to persons belonging to scheduled tribes.*

The *third aspect* concerns the responsibility of LAMPS in enrolling members. It has been found that in many LAMPS membership has remained virtually stagnant over many years and the actual membership is far less than potential members. Tribals are illiterate, by and large, and they lack knowledge regarding benefits a co-operative institution can provide and the nature of its functioning. In such a situation, it is natural that they will not come forward to enrol themselves as members of LAMPS. *It should be paramount duty of all LAMPS to conduct a survey of potential members in their area of operation and to make sincere efforts to enrol them as members.* This will definitely go a long way in making the society strong and viable.

Administration

LAMPS can improve their performance if administrative apparatus is made effective. Efficiency in administration is a factor to be developed at different stages. It is necessary to have a common pattern in different aspects of administration in LAMPS.

First, each LAMPS should consist of a *minimum number* of elected tribal directors of 7 or 8. The remaining among the prescribed number of directors should be filled by the government in the way of appointing ex-officio directors. The system of having elected directors and ex-officio directors is common in all the states. But the number varies as the policy in different states differs and also because the area of operation of LAMPS varies. If each LAMPS is organised in such a way as to cover one tehsil or block, there can be a common pattern so far as the number of directors is concerned. Each LAMPS should consist of a committee of management with eleven directors. Of the eleven directors, minimum of seven should be elected among tribal members and the rest should be ex-officio, who are closely associated with the working of LAMPS.

Four ex-officio directors to be appointed by the government should be from different concerned departments, such as one from forest department, one from co-operation department, one nominee of the financing bank and another officer belonging to social welfare department or integrated tribal development plan programme. All these four are stake holders in LAMPS. It is the forest department which is responsible to lease out forest area to LAMPS and to collect royalty, co-operation department has control and supervisory powers over LAMPS as enunciated in the Co-operative Societies Act, financing bank has a distinct say in the financial affairs of LAMPS, and department of social welfare or integrated tribal development plan has its own stake in that it is directly involved in tribal sub-plan strategy.

There may be states and union territories where scheduled castes persons are also enrolled as members of LAMPS. Since in a model LAMPS membership is restricted only to the scheduled tribes, it will be the natural corollary that elected directors will be only from among scheduled tribes members.

One of the important principles of co-operation is democratic control. Thus one of the essential requirements is that only elected member has to head the committee of management. In the case of LAMPS, if the elected tribal member is made the president of the society, it goes a long way in fulfilling the dream of tribal empowerment. In some of the societies, officers of government departments, particularly of forest department have been Presidents of LAMPS. This practice is in clear violation of the principle of democratic control and the aspirations of tribal empowerment.

Views differ on this aspect. Two of the four deputy conservators of forests and four of the seven other officers interviewed held the opinion that it will be better for the society if the president is an officer belonging to the forest department. Surprisingly, 82 of the 136 sample tribals and four of the 13 secretaries from whom the opinion was collected also favoured official President. The broad reasons cited in favour of their argument for having an officer of the forest department as president are mainly two. First, LAMPS is a forest based society and it is dependent on the forest department for different things such as to get the lease, to obtain passes to enter forests for MFP collections and to get permits to transport MFP etc. It is the forest department which fixes the royalty, decides which area or range has to be allotted to a certain LAMPS for MFP collection etc. Thus, association of LAMPS with the forest department is very close. If the President is an officer of this department the society can be unusually helped. The proponents of this view argue that wherever the DCFs or ACFs were Presidents of LAMPS, those societies have done the best in MFP activity and earnings of revenues. Second, their argument runs on the lines that LAMPS is basically a tribal society and a large section of tribals is illiterate and lacks knowledge of undertaking any business or of getting services from the society, their only purpose being working from dawn to dusk to eke out livelihood. Thus they hold the view that tribals are incapable of managing the affairs of the society, and under the Presidentship of a non-official person the society cannot fare well and it will collapse sooner or later.

But a study of the functioning of many LAMPS in Karnataka which have elected tribal members as Presidents has amply revealed that the above arguments do not hold water. These societies have been doing remarkably good business and have been able to rope in the forest department in the affairs of the society and to be in good terms with the officers of that department. Though it is little true that officers of the forest department favour the society if they are made president, the argument that he alone can turn the tables in favour of the society and the society should have an official president for ever is specious.

The principle of democratic control, the provisions of the co-operative societies Act and aspirations of tribal empowerment necessitate that the post of President of LAMPS should be held by an elected member. The claim that the tribals lack ability to manage the affairs of LAMPS properly has not been actually tested and proved. Inspite of this there are some views that an officer of the forest department should hold the post of President for a period of one or two years before an elected member takes over and in this intervening period tribals can be properly taught about the affairs of the society including MFP activity. This view seems to be reasonable. In the new LAMPS to be formed it should be mandatory that DCF or ACF of the area should hold the post of President for two years in the beginning and an elected President has to take over soon after that period. In these two years period of Presidentship of the officer, honest efforts should be made to improve the abilities of tribals by educating them. Necessary provisions in this regard should be included in the byelaws of the society.

Activity

LAMPS are by definition multi-purpose. Thus it is visualised and expected that they have to undertake varied and a large number of activities. The Bawa committee's concept that these institutions should cater to all the needs of the tribal people and should act as vehicles of tribal development necessarily entrusts a lot of responsibilities on LAMPS. Since these societies are formed and developed as part of the tribal sub-plan strategy and are supposed to assist tribals to fulfil their credit and marketing needs, it is natural that they take up a good number of activities. This approach will help the LAMPS on the one hand, to serve the tribals effectively, one of the most neglected section of people in the society and on the other, to earn reasonable amount of profit. And this will actually be in consonance with the principles of co-operation.

But there are many sections of people who articulate that LAMPS should not take up a number of activities and their business should be limited to MFP extraction and sale. Their view is that LAMPS are basically forest based societies for tribal people and as such it is pertinent that they should concentrate only on MFP activities, and that there are governmental agencies and other co-operative institutions to undertake other activities such as provision of credit, distribution of rationed goods, sale of consumer articles and agricultural inputs and so on. They argue that LAMPS are saddled with activities which are just allocative and not co-operative in nature They cite the examples of distribution of rationed food grains, supply of consumer articles to hostels and other designated institutions and provision of loans to member beneficiaries under some government sponsored schemes.

But this argument cannot be accepted. The view that LAMPS are engaged in a large number of activities which they are not supposed to do is myopic. All the activities undertaken by LAMPS so far are co-operative in nature. Provision of credit and collection and sale of MFP are directly co-operative in nature. Though the activities of distribution of rationed articles, sale of consumer articles and supply of goods to designated institutions contain an element of allocation in them, they are perfectly based on the principle of co-operative business.

It is to be admitted that a majority of the LAMPS in Karnataka and also in other states undertook the function of providing loans under integrated rural development programme and some other government sponsored schemes. But this activity was undertaken by LAMPS only in one or two years but was given up by some LAMPS after they burnt their fingers. Our observations and available data have shown that many LAMPS undertook the task of distributing medium-term loans under integrated rural development scheme to tribal beneficiaries. Under this scheme, all the concerned LAMPS normally sanctioned loans for bullock and cart. Each LAMPS in Karnataka had sanctioned loans to about 15 persons under this scheme. Loan portion of the money was availed from the concerned district central co-operative bank and subsidy was doled out by the government. But the LAMPS in Karnataka had the worst experience under this scheme. This was true with regard to the LAMPS of other states also. In Karnataka, about 80 percent of the loans sanctioned under this scheme was not repaid by members and the LAMPS had to repay the loan with interest out of their funds to the district central co-operative banks. A large number of LAMPS did not undertake this function henceforth. Thus, it should not be understood that LAMPS are still undertaking this activity which is almost a political function.

We strongly hold the view that LAMPS should not restrict their activities to just one or two but should diversify their business. It is advisable for them to *undertake a large number of activities so as to further the cause of tribal welfare as also to earn a good deal of profits.* Our view is based on three important grounds explained here under.

First, LAMPS are co-operative institutions and as such they are required to undertake business with a service motive as also with the intention of earning operative profits. Co-operative business cannot be restricted to any one activity. A true co-operative institution should be able to serve the members perfectly and effectively. In the modern world, co-operative institutions are stretching out and are taking up activities which were not traditionally in their fold.

Second, LAMPS are forest-based tribal societies, and by nature and definition they are multi-purpose. Other types of co-operatives may not be functioning in the area of operation of the LAMPS and even if there exist other co-operatives, tribals might not be their members. In other words, LAMPS are required to serve the tribal members in fulfillment of their economic needs. This amply explains why these institutions should not restrict their activities to just one or two.

Third, in the era of economic liberalisation and globalsiation, LAMPS are expected to withstand competition and to serve the members in a better way. They can neglect expanding the business activities only at their peril.

In this background we would like to propose different activities that can be undertaken by LAMPS.

First, LAMPS are entrusted with the function and responsibility of creating employment opportunities for members and show them avenues of income-generating activities. Thus, collection and sale of minor forest produces should be the major and the most important activity the LAMPS should undertake. Tribals live in forest and hill areas which bear different types of minor forest produces. Collection and sale of MFP has been the work of the tribals for centuries together. LAMPS have to utilize this to their best advantage. By procurement and sale of MFP, LAMPS will be handling a major income generating activity. But the LAMPS should be able to get better marketing facilities for these produces. An effective arrangement with LAMPS Federation, Tribal Development Corporation, Forest Development Corporation etc., whichever exists in a particular state, should be developed by LAMPS to sell the MFP they procure. It is essential that these federations or corporations should evolve a proper working arrangement with the TRIFED, New Delhi, to which they can sell the produce.

Second, an important activity that can be linked with MFP business is advancing of consumption loans. It has been found that no LAMPS in Karnataka has undertaken this activity so far. Advancing of consumption loans to the needy members to the extent of Rs. 1,000 to Rs. 1,500 will help the members a lot at the time of distress. This amount with proper rate of interest can be deducted in instalments at source, i.e., when the member sells MFP. It is necessary that the loan should be advanced based on proper security and credit worthiness of the borrower. This is because if the member fails to sell MFP to LAMPS, the latter should not be placed in a helpless position to recover the loan.

Enquiries of members across many LAMPS in Karnataka by this author have revealed that on a rough estimate about 55 per cent of them needed this type of loans. In the LAMPS where short-term and medium-term loans are advanced on a large scale, members were found to be not very much in need of consumption loans. But in other LAMPS members are very much in need of some kind of loan.

The system of advancing consumption loans to members and recovering them out of the surplus agricultural produce or MFP sold by members of LAMPS is in vogue and is perfectly working in Maharashtra. The Maharashtra State Tribal Development Corporation has entered into agreement with all the Adivasi Co-operative Societies authorising them to act as sub-agents to distribute consumption loans to needy members. Adivasi Co-operative Societies advance loans to members given by the tribal development corporation and recover out of the surplus agricultural produce or MFP sold by the member. The loan so recovered with interest is then passed on to the MSC TDC. Consumption loan of upto Rs. 2,000 is advanced to each tribal member in Maharashtra. It is found that recovery of loans under this scheme has been to the extent of 68 per cent.

Third, a large section of the members of LAMPS are agriculturists—usually small and marginal farmers. As any other agriculturist in the economy, tribal farmers also require loans. Thus it is necessary on the part of the LAMPS to advance short-term and medium-term loans to member-farmers to raise crops, to dig wells, to purchase and install pumpsets, for fencing, for reclamation of land and so on. LAMPS can also advance long-term loans to farmers as any commercial bank or co-operative bank does. Only one LAMPS in Karnataka has taken up this task. It has been observed that recovery of short-term, medium-term and long-term loans advanced by LAMPS is above 80 per cent except in the state of Orissa. Good percentage of recovery is ensured as these loans help asset creation and are normally advanced to members who are credit worthy and on the security of land and other properties. Thus, LAMPS in general should take up the venture of advancing short-term, medium term and long-term finances to agriculturist members.

Fourth, Banking activities, if taken up properly and with caution, will be definitely profitable to the institution and helpful to the public. Our observations have brought out the fact that a majority of LAMPS which have undertaken this activity possess proper expertise to do this. By advancing loans under different schemes, the LAMPS will be able to deploy their funds profitably. LAMPS should undertake this activity as any bank does. In other words, LAMPS should engage in banking activities by opening it to the general public and not restricting it only to their members.

Fifth, sale of 'non-controlled consumer commodities is one area where the LAMPS can expect a good profit margin. By taking up this activity they get an opportunity towards business expansion. 19 LAMPS in Karnataka and a large number of them in other states have been doing this business and their experience in this is really encouraging. Tribals live in remote villages, podus and forest areas and hence are rendered incapable to tread the path miles together to reach out to a shop or sales outlet to purchase consumer goods. Sales of consumer articles in the village branches of LAMPS not only helps the tribals but also goes a long way in recognising the valuable service of LAMPS.

Sixth, distribution of rationed articles helps the LAMPS to have a good deal of business. But there is an apprehension that this business fails to yield an operative profit margin and this function is just allocative in nature which can very well be handled by any governmental agency. But it is to be recognised that this business is allocative as well as co-operative in nature. It is not out of context to note that the government has recognised co-operative institutions as the best agencies to undertake distribution of controlled (rationed) commodities. It is a matter of pride to observe that co-operatives in India have not belied this expectation.

LAMPS have been distributing the allocated articles both to members and non-members in the area, both happen to be ration card holders. Enquiries and observations have conclusively revealed that this business yields 5 to 6 per cent profit margin. Again, this function will enable the LAMPS to have a close contact with their members. Services of LAMPS will be recognised by non-member card holders also.

Seventh, it has been the policy of the government to entrust the work of supply of food grains and other consumable articles to designated institutions in the taluka or a specific area to certain co-operative institutions like LAMPS, consumer's wholesale stores, agricultural produce co-operative marketing societies, etc. These designated institutions are normally hostels belonging to social welfare and backward classes and minorities departments and tribal welfare centres. LAMPS should not hesitate, in fact they should vie with other institutions and agencies to grab this opportunity of handling a lucrative business. Our observations in the LAMPS of Karnataka have revealed that, in many societies, nearly half of their total business consists of this activity. And in a few LAMPS this business is to the extent of even 60 per cent of the total business handled by them. Available data have conclusively indicated that this business yields a profit margin of not less than 8 per cent.

Again, handling of this business does not need much and extraordinary expertise. Our enquiries with the authorities of LAMPS in Karnataka and some other states have made us come to the conclusion that supplies to designated institutions are a very lucrativce business which also provide a good deal of recognition to them. Hence, a model LAMPS should be able to expand its activities by undertaking this type of business.

Eighth, in this most competitive world and the era of gloablisation and economic liberalisation, it is essential for any enterprise to diversify its activities to sustain in the business. This principle applies even to LAMPS many of which are still in the early stages of existence. LAMPS are advised to undertake business activities considering the local needs. Sale of fertilisers and other agricultural inputs, cloth and so on is done by a handful of LAMPS in Karnataka and outside. But undertaking this business cannot be the common principle or strategy. For example, only a very small section of tribal farmers have adopted improved agricultural methods and are growing cash crops. Our observations in many LAMPS have revealed that, they depend upon the concerned governmental departments to get fertilisers and improved seeds. In such a situation, selling of fertilisers in a branch of LAMPS is perilous and no body with a business mind will definitely undertake such a business. But it is to be admitted that there are many LAMPS which are thriving in the business of sale of cloth, fertilisers etc., All that can be suggested is LAMPS should undertake and expand their business by considering local needs of the area.

Conclusion

A model LAMPS should think of furthering the cause of tribal welfare as well as earning of a good profit margin to sustain and grow. In the true spirit of a co-operative, it should have both service motive and profit motive.

LAMPS should act as real agents of tribal development and tribal empowerment. This necessitates expansion of their vision.

Living in abandoned, remote, hilly and forest areas, tribal people are easily prone to many diseases. They lack a sense of understanding the significance of human development, health care and literacy. Our visits to and observations at Swami Vivekananda Youth Movement at Heggadadevanakote and Vivekananda Girijana Kalyana Kendra at B.R. Hills have revealed that these institutions are very much involved in tribal development and tribal welfare. LAMPS can lend a helping hand to such institutions wherever they exist. Even in places where such organisations do not exist, LAMPS can actively take up the programmes of health care, mass education, imparting knowledge of modern agricultural practices etc. This will do its best to establish that LAMPS are institutions which take care of tribal welfare in its broader sense.

CHAPTER — 6

Building Powerful Tribal Co-operatives

Large-sized Adivasi Multi-purpose Co-operative Societies have been organised in India with the objective of bringing about transformation in the tribal economy. Many programmes and policies have been implemented for tribal welfare during different plans in India and establishment of LAMPS is an important step in the measures for tribal development. These societies were thought of to be organised according to the recommendations of the study team headed by K.S. Bawa, Joint Secretary in the Ministry of Co-operation, Government of India, since 1974. Institutions which were existing then in the name of Forest Labour Societies were renamed as, and a large number of societies were formed afresh nomenclatured as LAMPS.

On the basis of the general view and the stark reality that tribal people are backward and also have been neglected economically, socially and culturally, tribal sub-plan was introduced in the country since 1974-75 to accord the most preferential treatment to that community.

LAMPS have been organised altogether in sixteen states and two union territories of the country. They were organised with the main objective of providing marketing opportunities for forest based and surplus agricultural produce of the tribals. LAMPS were expected to be harbingers of change in the tribal system. Over a quarter century of their existence, LAMPS have gone a long way in moulding the tribal economy. But the performance of majority of LAMPS is still not upto the desired level.

Major Findings

1. Even though LAMPS were organised with the aim of bringing about a thorough transformation in the tribal economy their performance, by and large, is not to the desired extent. These institutions have found their existence in sixteen states and two union territories of India. But their performance is just satisfactory only in some pockets of Madhya Pradesh, Karnataka, Tamil Nadu, Maharashtra and north-eastern states. Needless to say, LAMPS have not been harbingers of change as expected when they were established as per Bawa Committee recommendation and as part of the tribal sub-plan strategy.
2. Uniformity in the organisational structure of LAMPS is lacking. As per the suggestions of the study team headed by K.S. Bawa, it was visualised to organise one LAMPS for each block or tehsil. But in practice it has not remained so. For example, in Maharashtra, three or four LAMPS are organised in each tehsil. In Orissa, 46 LAMPS exist with an area of operation of one block or tehsil each and the remaining societies are organised at the rate of 2 or 3 per block. In

Karnataka, two LAMPS each have three talukas and one LAMPS has two talukas in their area of operation, and the remaining LAMPS are organised at the rate of one per tehsil. Hence, LAMPS have been organised or restructured to suit the local conditions and needs.

3. Structure of management in LAMPS is not uniform among different states and even among different districts in some states. For example, in Orissa state, each LAMPS has in its board 18 directors of whom 15 are elected and the remaining are nominees of the government. In Karnataka, though each LAMPS consists of eleven directors, constitution of the board with elected directors and ex-officio directors is not uniform between one district and the other. Number of elected directors varies from six to nine and ex-officio directors from two to five in different districts. Even though LAMPS were organised with a clear agenda and were visualised with a national perspective to cater to the needs of a certain section of population which is scattered in different parts across the country, uniformity in the structure of management of these institutions is evidently absent.

4. LAMPS are by name and in deed, co-operative institutions for tribal people. In the recommendations of the Bawa Committee and strategy of the tribal sub-plan, they are visualised as institutions to cater to the needs of only tribal community. But in some states and in one union territory even persons belonging to scheduled castes have been enrolled as members of these societies. The view, perhaps may be that, scheduled caste people are also a neglected lot

and are backward socially, economically and culturally, it would not be inappropriate to enrol them as members along with scheduled tribes people. But it is to be noted that if scheduled castes persons also find a place as members, the true nature and the spirit of LAMPS as adivasi society will take a back seat.

5. With regard to another important managerial aspect i.e., recruitment of the chief executive, there is no similarity in LAMPS. For example, in Maharashtra, Secretary of LAMPS is an employee of the State Tribal Development Corporation, in North-Eastern States he is recruited by the society itself, in Orissa he is an officer of the government usually a Senior Inspector of Co-opertive Societies, and in Tamil Nadu, he is a paid Secretary recruited by the society itself. Karnataka State presents a different picture with three types of Chief Executives existing in its 21 LAMPS. That is, Chief Executives are recruited by the committee of management itself in the case of some LAMPS, they are deputed by the government to work in these institutions for a certain term in the case of a few LAMPS, and in a few other LAMPS Chief Executive is just in the in-charge position, and is drawing salary and emoluments from the government.

The name of the designation of Chief Executive is also different in different states and also within the state. For example, the name of the designation is 'Managing Director' in Orissa, 'Secretary' in Maharasthra, Tamil Nadu and North-Eastern states. In Karnataka, the name of the designation is 'Secretary' in 18 LAMPS, 'Manager' in one LAMPS and 'Managing Director' in two LAMPS.

6. By and Large, LAMPS have failed to make a dent in tribal life. Even after half a century of their existence, in many parts of the country LAMPS are groping in the dark as to what activities they have to undertake and in what way to run the enterprise. In Orissa, LAMPS have virtually gone into red. Many of the societies there are on the verge of liquidation. In Tamil Nadu, participation of LAMPS in MFP activity in minuscule. Only a few out 11 LAMPS are engaged in collection and sale of MFP. Majority of the LAMPS there have not dared to take up this activity owing to paucity of funds. Instead, they have taken up the activities of lending term loans and jewel loans. In Bihar, the tale of LAMPS is almost the same as that in Orissa. In Maharasthra, only because LAMPS are restructured by narrowing down their area of operation and linking them directly with the state tribal development corporation, they have been able to do their worth. LAMPS have stood their ground and have been doing a humble and praiseworthy service in some parts of Madhya Pradesh, i.e., in Bastar and Jagadalpur areas. Performance of these institutions in Karnataka State is mixed. Only about half of the total societies have been able to diversify their activities and to earn accumulated profits. Almost the same is the story in north-eastern states where LAMPS have undertaken a number of activities and a large number of LAMPS have been functioning on an operative profit.

It can be said that the organisation of LAMPS in many states of India has not gone a long way in bringing about a social and economic transformation of the tribal system.

7. It has been found in some parts of the country that tribal members do not sell MFP and surplus agricultural produce to the LAMPS. Instead, they sell them to private traders. This is owing to the fact that LAMPS are not easily accessible to members as well as existence of a sort of communication gap between the society and the members about collection, sale and price of the produce. Tribals may find it easy to sell away the produce to private traders who come and collect it on down payment. Orissa's example may serve to explain the situation. In that State, LAMPS are supposed to sell their produce to the state tribal development corporation on getting advance payment. But of late, TDC is not coming forward to make advance payments to LAMPS since many of these societies are unviable. Thus LAMPS are left with no funds to make payment for the produce which the tribal sells. Hence, the functioning of LAMPS in many pockets of the country has not made the things any better. This again proves that the tribal people have not been able to reap the benefits that the LAMPS are expected to provide.

8. Actual membership in the LAMPS is not to the desired extent. In Karnataka, the actual membership in most of these societies is less than 50 percent of the potential members. As has been observed by this author, the same is the case in Orissa, Tamil Nadu, Maharashtra and Bihar. Thus, LAMPS have failed to build up a sound organisational structure and to develop working capital base by attracting shareholders. A large section of the eligible tribals have been left out of the membership of LAMPS. By selling their produce to the private traders, tribals are

deprived of the benefit of a better and fair price which they could have got if they had sold it to LAMPS. It was found in many parts the price that tribals get for the produce from traders is just about 40 percent of what they could have obtained at LAMPS.

9. Even though LAMPS are well entrenched in tribal life in many pockets of many states, they have not been able to make the best of their efforts. LAMPS normally make some advance payment to tribal collectors which will be deducted and the remaining amount paid when the produce is delivered. Only some LAMPS in the country advance term loans and in Maharasthra, Consumption finance is advanced as a scheme of the state tribal development corporation. Thus a system of loaning, repayment, savings etc., is not developed in the tribal system and tribal economy is still largely a non-monetised one.

10. In order to have an effective system of working of LAMPS, particularly in the activity of collection and sale of minor forest produces, proper organisational link is of utmost importance. But it was found that in majority of states this link was either lacking or totally absent.

An effective organisational link among different tiers in the system is essential. LAMPS at the primary level are engaged in collection of MFP from the tribals. They in turn have to sell the produce to state level organisations such as tribal development corporations, LAMPS federations or state forest development corporations. The produce is to be marketed at the national level at TRIFED or other agencies. But in actual practice, this supposed system is not properly working. For example, in Orissa, the State

Tribal Development Corporation has miserably failed to leave an imprint on tribal activities. A large section of people are really unaware of the functioning and business handled by T.D.C. Since majority of the LAMPS are unviable and have lost financial credibility, TDC has developed cold feet to make advance payments to LAMPS. As a result, a large quantity of MFP is sold by tribals to private traders and TDC also is purchasing from these traders. TDC in Bihar is virtually defunct. Hence, it has failed to coordinate the activities of LAMPS. In Maharashtra, the State Tribal Development Corporation is no doubt doing a very good job. But even here, some of the produce is sold by tribals to private traders, and TDC has not developed cordial trade relations with TRIFED. In Karnataka, LAMPS federation is in infant stage, and the business of procuring MFP from LAMPS and marketing it at TRIFED has just started. Hence, its working and the results are yet to be seen. The situation in Madhya Pradesh is not different from what exists in Orissa and Bihar. But only in the last three years there has been a change in Bastar and Jagdalpur parts of the state when TRIFED itself volunteered to purchase from the LAMPS and to ensure a fair price for the produce. A different picture emerges in Tamil Nadu where state level federation does not exist and the LAMPS, whichever are engaged in collection of MFP, are directly linked with the TRIFED.

11. One of the important objectives with which the LAMPS were organised was to provide employment opportunities to tribals and to enhance their income-earning capacity. LAMPS might have succeeded in fulfilling this purpose to a small extent. But, by and large, their failure is evident. In a large number of LAMPS contact between the society and the member virtually does not exist. LAMPS, instead of purchasing the

produce directly from the members, purchase through middlemen or agents. This negates co-operative character of the LAMPS. This has two important and far-reaching connotations. First, it leaves the tribal with the belief that he sells the produce to a trader or a private person and that he has nothing to do with the LAMPS. Second, the tribal collector is deprived of the full price or the fair price for the produce, since some amount of money in the form of commission is pocketed by the middlemen.

12. LAMPS in India are established and developed largely with the financial assistance of the government. This assistance is being routed to the LAMPS in several forms such as share capital, subsidy, loan, margin money, etc. The present study reveals that each LAMPS in the country has been able to obtain several lakhs of Rupees of assistance in these forms. Financial assistance to these institutions is not restricted to any single year. In fact it is given in a number of years. Thus, government itself has the status of a share holder in LAMPS. LAMPS cannot think of their existence in the absence of this largesse doled out by the government. The scheme of providing share capital assistance to LAMPS in order to admit members is in vogue in many states. This scheme was in operation in Karnataka only till 1996. According to this scheme, the amount of share capital to be subscribed by the member, share fee and admission fee is given by the government. Thus, becoming a share holder does not impose any financial burden on the part of the tribal person! These factors show that the real spirit of co-operation is not enshrined in the functioning of LAMPS as they are largely

organised with governmental assistance and patronage.

13. Everything for the LAMPS in their business is not easy. The problems they face can very well be seen in their MFP activity. LAMPS have to face many hurdles while obtaining lease from the forest department. Undue delay in granting lease causes heavy loss of revenue to the LAMPS. Even after the lease is granted, LAMPS come across many restrictions to collect MFP. Many a time, morale of LAMPS is badly affected.

14. Some minor forest produces are not fully harvested. Tree mass provides the best example for this which is harvested only to the extent of 10 per cent of the availability. Tribals show inclination to collect those produces the harvesting of which is easy.

15. LAMPS across the country have not given importance to sustainable harvesting and optimum level of harvesting. Some of the produces like Amla require about 15 to 20 per cent to be left in the plant so that it helps regeneration. But tribals are easily given to the temptation to harvest the whole crop with commercial motive. Honey is extracted cutting the whole beehive and also affecting bees and larvae. With the dwindling forest cover and depleting quantum of produces on the one hand, and increasing tribal population on the other, it may be difficult in the future to avail the same level and quantum of produces. Unless LAMPS attach due importance to train and educate their members about sustainable and optimum level of harvesting, their motive of increasing employment opportunities and income generation among

tribals will prove to be self-defeating. In the absence of sustainable harvesting, eco-system and ecological balance will be in danger which badly affects tribal living.

16. Social performance of the LAMPS is poor indeed. As said earlier, actual membership in majority of these societies is far less than the potential members. Participation of members in general body meetings and also in activities of LAMPS is very less.

17. Agricultural labourers and marginal farmers predominate among the members of LAMPS. This leads us to the conclusion that tribals by and large are very poor and economically backward.

18. Activities of a very large number of LAMPS are in consonance with the recommendations of the study team headed by K.S. Bawa. That is, they have been undertaking various activities such as, marketing of minor forest and agricultural produce, distribution of inputs and consumer goods and provision of credit.

19. In Karnataka as well as in other states processing activity is not developed on a large scale. This activity is almost a neglected one. If the processing activity is given due importance, LAMPS will be able to make value addition to the commodity and sell at a higher price. This will enhance the capacity of the society to earn more profits and to serve the members in an effective way. In Karnataka, only three LAMPS have got processing units which are functioning. One LAMPS has set up a unit very recently. Processing units of two LAMPS have virtually stopped functioning long ago. In other states also only a

handful of LAMPS have processing units of their own. This situation has made the LAMPS sell the raw produce at a very low price and forego the profit margin which they could have earned, if they had the facility to process and market the commodity.

20. In many cases LAMPS have been working as governmental agencies. A huge amount of funds to these societies in the form of share capital, margin money, subsidy, loan etc., is being given under various schemes by the government. Apart from this, government has been gracious enough to allocate many functions to LAMPS such as distribution of rationed goods and supply of consumer articles and food grains to designated institutions. These have become main activities of many LAMPS. Thus these societies are at the mercy of the government and are not in a position to think of their existence if these allocative functions are withdrawn. Again, as in other fields of cooperation, in this field of tribal co-operation also, members' awareness about the role of the society and its function is at the lowest. A large number of members are under the impression that LAMPS is just an institution of the government.

21. LAMPS have a weak financial structure. Much of their funds is provided by the government in the form of share capital, loans and subsidy. Amount of Government's share predominates and in the case of many LAMPS it is to the extent of more than 90 per cent out of the total share capital of the society. LAMPS are running their show out of the funds given by the government.

Organisational base of the LAMPS also is weak. Majority of the directors of the board are incapable of taking decisions and understanding the issues at large. The most horrible and an unimaginable factor is that majority of the ex-officio directors do not attend board meetings. It is a pity that persons who have been directors by virtue of their office and who are carefully chosen to represent the government on the board have taken the things for granted and have shown utter contempt about the activities and administration of tribal societies.

Recommendations

In the light of our present study, it is deemed fit to make the following recommendations, in order to make the LAMPS robust.

1. It will be appropriate on the part of LAMPS to have membership to the maximum possible extent. As these societies are organised specially to cater to all the needs of tribals, and only a small number of tribals have taken membership in other co-operative societies in the area of operation of LAMPS, it is pertinent on their part to admit all potential members and find ways to serve them. LAMPS should undertake a survey to identify tribal families and potential members, i.e. those tribals who have attained 18 years of age, in their area of operation. In cases where tribals do not come forward to enrol as members, attempts should be made by the LAMPS to attract them towards the society and admit them as members. LAMPS should arrange meetings of tribals where they can educate them about the importance of becoming members of these societies. Assistance of state co-operative federations and district co-operative unions should be elicited in this endeavour. Office bearers of the LAMPS, both elected and paid, should evince keen interest in enrolling new

members. Increased membership enhances working capital base as well as responsibilities of the society.

2. It has been found that in several states and in the union territory of Dadra and Nagar Haveli, persons belonging to scheduled castes are also enrolled as members of LAMPS. They have found representation on the board of directors also. But LAMPS by name and in deed is a society for adivasis i.e., tribals. Thus it is of utmost importance to enrol only persons belonging to scheduled tribes as members of LAMPS.

3. It is necessary that the LAMPS have to be organised in conformity with the suggestions of the Bawa Committee. Each LAMPS should be organised having one tehsil or block as its area of operation and it can be served with as many number of branches as required. These branches may serve as sales outlets and collection centres. Thus, uniformity in the organisation and area of operation of LAMPS is essential to bring about effectiveness in their services and to avoid any sort of overlapping in their activities.

4. For an effective and result-oriented functioning of LAMPS, they should be linked with two higher levels of organisations, i.e., at the state and the national level. It was a suggestion of the Bawa Committee that "suitable higher level organisations should be pressed into service to support, supervise and guide the activities of societies at the primary level".[1] To provide better marketing for the produces procured by LAMPS, organisations at the higher levels are essential. In the absence of these organisations, LAMPS have to fall back upon private traders to sell

their produce, a system which cuts at the very root of these societies. Hence, the system of procurement and marketing of tribal produce should be a three tier structure—LAMPS at the primary level, state level federation at the middle level and national level organisation at the apex level. TRIFED at the national level has been rendering a very good service in the field. State level federations are to be established wherever they are not existing.

5. Since LAMPS is a co-operative institution exclusively for tribal people, the President/ Chairman should invariably be a tribal non-official person. But as we have advocated in the chapter 'A Model for LAMPS', in the beginning for a period of two years, an official usually a forest officer can be chosen as President so that in the intervening period members of LAMPS could have sufficient opportunities to obtain minimum knowledge about co-operative business and activities of the society.

6. In the three tier structure at present, the middle level organisations are not functioning properly and have lost creditability in many states. Hence they have utterly failed to motivate LAMPS and to show proper direction to them. In Bihar and Orissa, state tribal development corporations have failed in fulfilling their aim and are almost defunct. In Maharasthra, TDC of course, is doing a good job but has shown its failure in developing cordial relations with LAMPS on the one hand and with TRIFED on the other. Hence the existing state level federations which are either defunct or have lost credibility should be rejuvenated or liquidated forthwith and new

Corporations/Federations have to be organised in their place. These federations may be different in different states such as LAMPS federation, tribal development corporation, etc., Unless the middle tier is strong and viable the whole structure will collapse.

7. It is advisable on the part of LAMPS to have paid Secretaries, i.e., Chief Executives recruited and paid by the Society itself. As has been narrated in Chapter III, paid Secretaries very well fit the bill and can wholeheartedly work for the betterment of the society. They will have full time at their disposal to involve themselves in the activities of LAMPS and at the same time they will be very much under the administrative control of the committee of management.

8. As suggested in the Bawa Committee report, LAMPS should concentrate their efforts in taking up a large number of activities so as to improve their competitiveness as well as to serve the members in a more effective way. Collection and sale of MFP, distribution of essential goods, supply of food grains and consumer articles to designated institutions such as hostels and tribal welfare centres, processing, training-cum-production work, banking etc., can be easily taken up by LAMPS. Financial support to take up these activities is easily forthcoming from government and other agencies. But it is advisable to engage only in those activities which earn sufficient rate of profits and which are really service-oriented.

9. Much of the problem for LAMPS in MFP activity is with the forest department. There is need for grant of fresh lease for forest area without any

delay, so as to allow the LAMPS to be in continuity with the earlier lease and to provide for an unhindered collection of MFP. Rules and regulations in the issuance of permits should be relaxed and the system is to be made easy so as to avoid any inconvenience to the tribal collector. It is essential also on the part of LAMPS that they must adhere to the rules and apply for fresh lease much before the existing lease period expires.

10. Forest produces are national wealth and tribal people are just usufruct beneficiaries. Thus, royalty or lease amount must be paid by the LAMPS to the government since the former has permitted to use national wealth with a profit motive. There are many arguments that the royalty system should be dispensed with and the LAMPS must be allowed to procure MFP free. The report of the National Commission on Agriculture had the view that ".....tribals be allowed to collect minor forest produce free of charge".[2]

It is the view of this author that the royalty should not be dispensed with and the system of payment of royalty by LAMPS to the forest department should be continued. Though forest resources are national wealth and can be obtained free of charge, they acquire a different dimension when they are extracted on a large scale and used for a commercial purpose. Without quid pro quo, extraction and usage of the produce will not have a tint of economic value and commercial venture. Only when the lease amount is paid, LAMPS will try to harvest the produce with a purpose and to the best of their advantage. This has many advantages such as maximum extraction of forest resources, increase in employment and income earning opportunities for tribals and enhancement of MFP revenues for LAMPS.

But what is advocated in the present study is a rebate by the government to the LAMPS to reduce the burden of payment of royalty on them. As LAMPS are engaged in the service of tribal community and have to encounter several problems in MFP collection the system of giving subsidy which can act as a rebate in the payment of royalty is essential. This system which was in existence till 1990 has to be given effect to again. We recommend a 50 per cent subsidy to the LAMPS by the government in lieu of payment of royalty to the forest department, so that LAMPS are left with only half of the burden.

But due care is needed to be taken to fix the royalty amount. It should be based on the area leased, availability of the produce and an average of previous five year's lease amount. This may prove to be most scientific method in fixing royalty.

At present, the lease period is for two years, after the expiry of which the society has to obtain fresh lease. This has proved to be inconvenient for the society. The society is expected to apply for fresh lease much in advance and necessary resolution has to be passed by the committee of management to this effect. Two year period is very less and in majority of cases LAMPS fail to apply for lease well in advance, and there is inordinate delay in granting lease by the forest department. Hence, what is strongly recommended is a five year lease period.

12. Even though there are more than 30 important items of MFP only a handful of them, that is about 12 to 15 produces have received much attention in extraction and sale. It is a general view that there may be many more minor forest produces in existence. Hence a thorough research

to find out the availability of MFP which might have still remained unknown is suggested.

13. Training of members of LAMPS must be given much importance. It is true that LAMPS have been imparting training to their members at present. But the way in which it is given now is of little use. Duties and responsibilities of members are taught in the training classes and members attend these classes half heartedly or only for the purpose of getting stipend. It is essential to impart vocational training which can help members to engage in productive activities. A large amount of expenditure of LAMPS should be on training programme and government's assistance and schemes have to be fully utilised in this regard. Efforts should be devoted to educate the members about their responsibilities and importance of their participation in the activities of the society as also to properly train them to take up productive activities utilising local resources. Emphasis should be laid also on the methods of sustainable harvesting of the produce.

14. One of the important aims of LAMPS is to create and increase employment opportunities for tribal people. It is not out of context to say that LAMPS should foster cottage industries and develop small scale village industries with the aim of utilising forest based resources to bring about an increase in production, income and employment. National commission on Agriculture had held the view that "forest based industries will have to be located in tribal areas for diversification of employment opportunities...".[3] LAMPS are the best agencies to take up this venture.

15. Many a tribal member will be in dire need of money and he has no institution to fall back upon except the LAMPS. It is necessary that LAMPS should take up the activity of advancing consumption loans and recover it in instalments either in cash or at source when the produce is sold to it. This activity in all the LAMPS can be developed on the model that exists in Maharashtra State where adivasi societies act as agents of TDC in distribution of consumption finance; or alternatively LAMPS can directly advance these loans out of their funds.

16. LAMPS, like any other co-operative institution, will function effectively only with proper participation of its members. These institutions are required to run on co-operative basis. The minimum they are expected to do is to pay dividend on the shares of members. It was found that majority of LAMPS have not bothered to declare and pay dividend on the shares held by members and government. Non-payment of dividend amounts to violation of the principle of co-operative business and also of the existing rules. Again, through payment of dividend, LAMPS can ensure better participation of members and can instill a feeling among members that they are also stake holders.

17. As we have seen in the study, attendance of official directors in the board meetings is negligible. Unless these directors actively participate in the activities of LAMPS and attend board meetings regularly, functioning and performance of LAMPS will not be to the expected level. Only the officers of departments which are closely connected with the activities of

LAMPS should be appointed as ex-officio directors on the committee of management of LAMPS and it is necessary on the part of the government to take such steps as to make these officers attend the meetings regularly.

18. It is true that attendance of elected directors in the board meetings is satisfactory. But to further improve their attendance and in order to make them actively participate in the activities of LAMPS and in decision making process, LAMPS can think of holding out some incentives to elected directors. Three aspects can be considered in this direction. They are (i) director's attendance in the board meetings and sub-committee meetings, (ii) their role in enrolment of new members, and (iii) their participation in increasing the volume of business. These factors should be taken into account to give incentives on an annual basis.

19. At present, LAMPS exist only in sixteen states and two union territories. But there are many other states and union territories in India which impocket a large section of tribal population. As has been found in the 1991 census, except for the states of Delhi, Haryana and Punjab and the union Territories of Chandigarh and Pondicherry, all other states and union Territories have tribal population in them. But tribal population in the two state of Goa is minuscule, being only 0.03 per cent of its total population. There is scope for organising LAMPS in other states having tribal population barring the State of Goa. Hence, the Government should come forward with a policy to organise and develop LAMPS in the States of Himachal Pradesh, Megalaya, Sikkim, and West

Bengal and in the Union Territories of Andaman and Nicobar Islands and Lakshadweep.

But we are not advocating organisation of LAMPS in Andhra Pradesh though the state has a large chunk of tribal population which is 6.31 per cent of its total population as per the census of 1991. This is because Girijan Co-operative Corporation, Andhra pradesh, has been doing an excellent job in the fields of collection and marketing of minor forest produces, supply of daily requirements to tribals and advancing of term loans. With a net work of 45 Girijan Primary Co-operative Marketing Societies which are working in the same way as LAMPS, and 817 daily requirement depots., the GCC is performing an unenviable task. Its working and success have a very great lesson. Its role and model are fit to be emulated.

REFERENCES

1. Government of India, Summary Report of the Study Team on Co-operative Structure in Tribal Development Agency projects, 1973, p. 3.
2. Government of India, Report of the National Commission on Agriculture, 1976, Part IX, Forestry, p. 152.
3. Ibid, p. 151.

BIBLIOGRAPHY

I. Books

1. Arun Bhandaikar, *Problems of Development of Tribal Areas,* Leeladevi Publications, New Delhi, 1980.
2. Bardhan, A.B. *The Tribal Problem in India,* Communist Party of India Publication - 12, New Delhi, 1976.
3. Budhadeb Chauduri, *Tribal Development in India,* Inter-India Publications, New Delhi, 1982.
4. Bhupinder Singh and Bhandari, J.S. (Ed.) *The Tribal World and its Transformation,* Concept Publishing Company, New Delhi, 1980.
5. Bose, S. *Tribal Life of India,* National Book Trust, New Delhi, 1971.
6. Dalton, G. (Ed.) *Tribal and Peasant Economics: Readings in Economic Anthropology,* University of Texas Press, Austin, 1967.
7. Dube, S.C. (Ed.) *Tribal Heritage of India,* Vikas Publications, New Delhi, 1977.
8. Ghurye, G.A. *The Scheduled Tribes,* G.R. Bhatkal, Bombay, 1963.
9. Kamala Devi Chattopadhyay, *Tribalism in India,* Vikas Publishing House, Sahidabad, 1978.
10. Kothari, K.L. *Tribal Social Change in India,* Himanshu Publications, New Delhi, 1985.
11. Kulkarni, M.G. *Problems of Tribal Development - A Case Study,* Parimal Prakashana, Aurangabad, 1974.

12. Mahalingam, S., *Role of Co-operative Organisations in Developing Tribal Economy,* Mittal Publications, New Delhi, 1990.

13. Mahalingam, S. Tribal Co-operative System - A Study of North-East India, Rawat Publications, Jaipur, Delhi, 1992.

14. Maheshwari Prasad (Ed.). *Tribes their Environment and Culture, Amar Prakashan,* Delhi, 1987.

15. Navinchandra Jain, Robin, D. Tribhuvan (Ed.). *An Overview of Tribal Research Studies,* Tribal Research and Training Institute, Pune, 1995.

16. Negi, P.S., *Social-Cultural Dynamics of Tribal Development,* Tribal Research and Training Institute, Maharashtra State, Pune.

17. Nadeem Mohsin, *Tribal Culture in a Flux,* B.R. Publishing Corporation, Delhi, 1977.

18. Pareek, R.N., *Tribal Culture in a Flux,* B.R. Publishing Corporation, Delhi, 1997.

19. Patel, M.L., *Agro-Economic Problems of Tribal India,* Progressive Book Depot, Bhopal, 1972.

20. Patnaik, N., *Tribals and their Development,* Hyderabad National Institute of Community Development, 1972.

21. Rajagopalan, R. (Ed.) *Rediscovering Co-operation,* Vol. II, *Strategies for the Models of Tomorrow,* Institute of Rural Management Anand, 1996.

22. Ramaiah, P., *Tribal Economy of India, Light and Life Publishers,* New Delhi.

23. Rana, J.M., *Multi-Purpose Co-operative Societies in South-East Asia,* International Co-operative Alliance, New Delhi, 1974.

24. Ranjit Gupta (Ed.), *Poverty and Quality of Life in a Tribal Area,* Ankur Publishing House, New Delhi, 1977.

25. Sarveshwara Rao and G. Parthasarathy (Ed.), *Regulated Markets and Public Policy.* Institute of Development and Planning Studies, Vishakapatnam, 1995.

26. Shukla, H.L., *Tribal History: A New Interpretation,* B.R. Publishing Corporation, Delhi, 1988.

27. Singh, K.S. (Ed.), *Economics of the Tribes and their transformation,* Concept Publishing Company, Delhi, 1982.

28. Sinha, S., *Tribes and their Development: A Study of Two Tribal Development Blocks in Orissa,* Bihar: Man in India, 1974.

29. Suresh Chandra Rajora, *Social Structure and Tribal Elites,* Himanshu Publications, New Delhi, 1987.

30. Tandon, B.C., Research Methodology in Social Sciences, Chaitanya Publishing House, Allahabad, 1979.

31. Trivedi, H.V., *Economic Development of Tribes in India,* Himanshu Publications, New Delhi, 1985.

32. Tushaar Shah, *Catalysing Co-operation,* Sate Publications, New Delhi, 1996.

33. Vidyarthi, L.P, and Pai, B.K., *The Tribal Culture of India,* Concept Publishing, Delhi.

34. Varier Elwin (Ed.) *A New Deal for Tribal India,* Publications Division, Ministery of Home Affairs, New Delhi, 1963.

35. Vyas, M.N. and Mann, R.S., *Indian Tribes in Transition,* Rawat Publications, Jaipur, Delhi, 1980.

II. Articles

1. Ajit Dange, A., "Co-operatives and Tribal Development", *The Co-operative,* Vol. XVIII, No. 5, September 1980.

2. Batra, J.D., "Tribal Co-operatives-Progress and Development", *The Co-operative,* Vol. XVII, No. 6, September 15, 1979.

3. Bhupinder Singh, "Tribal Development", *The Newsletter,* Vol. III, No. 1, and 2, April 1982.

4. Bhupinder Singh, "Co-operatives in Tribal Areas", Occasional Papers on Tribal Development, Ministry of Home Affairs, Government of India, 1983.

5. Bhupinder Singh, "*The Tribal Problem - Some Reflections*" (Unpublished Paper).

6. Gogoi, D.K., "Hill Areas of Assam Touch New Economic Hights", *Yojana,* Vol. XXIV, NO. 23, December 16-13, 1980.

7. Gopalan, M., and Kali, V., "LAMPS - A Micro Study", *Kurukshetra,* June 1998.

8. Gupta, M.C., "Co-operation in Tribal Areas", *The Co-operator,* Vol. XXII, No. 16, February 15, 1985.

9. Guru, H.N., "Tribal Co-operatives in Madchya Pradesh: The LAMPS", *The Co-operator,* Vol. XXI, No. 20, April 15, 1984.

10. Lakshman Reddy, T., "Strategy of Developing Hill and Tribal Areas through Co-operative Movement", *Indian Co-operative Review,* Vol. XII, No. 2, January 1975.

11. Manzoor Ahmed, "Tribal Development through Co-operatives", *The Co-operator,* Vol. XVII, No. 6, September 15, 1979.

12. Maurya, B.P., "Development of the Tribals", *Co-operative News Digest,* Vol. XXVI, January 1975.

13. Mehta, V.L., "Problems of Tribal People", *Khadi Gramodyog,* Vol. 5, January 1959.

14. Mishra, R.K., "Co-operative Sector as an Instrument of Economic Change in Tribal and Hill Areas", *Indian Co-operative Review,* Vol. XII, No. 2, January 1975.

15. Naidu, Y.N., "Scheduled Tribes: Exploited by Co-operatives", *Economic and Political Weekly,* Bombay, 1975.

16. Omprakash Mehra, "Strategy for Tribal Development", *The Indian Journal of Public Administration,* Vol. XXIII, No. 3, 1977.

17. Puri, V.K., "Planning for Tribal Development", *Yojana,* Vol. XXII, No. 10, June 1, 1978.

18. Roy Burman, B.K., "Issues in Tribal Development", (unpublished paper).

19. Sanjay Kumar Verma, "Co-operatives: Harbinger of Change in Baster", *The Co-operator,* July 1999.

20. Sharchchandra Lele, "Darkness under LAMPS", *Deccan Herald,* May 18, 1996.

21. Sharma, B.D., "Planning from below with Special References to Tribal Areas", Occasional papers on Tribal

Development, - 10, Ministry of Home Affairs, Government of India, New Delhi, 1977.

22. Sharma, K.S., "Agro-Forest Based Industries for Accelerated Growth of Tribals", *Indian Co-operative Review,* Vol. XII, No. 2, January 1975.

23. Yoginder Singh Verma and Kulwant Singh Pathania, "Performance of Co-operative Movement in Tribal Areas of Himachal Pradesh", *The Co-operator,* Vol. XXIV, No. 12, December 15, 1986.

III. Reports, Documents and Hand Books

1. Government of India, Ministry of Home Affairs, New Delhi, *Census of India,* 1991.

2. Government of India, *Census of India,* 1991, *Final Population Totals, Figures at a Glance, Karnataka State.*

3. Government of India, Ministry of Agriculture and Irrigation, New Delhi, *Report of the National Commission on Agriculture,* 1976, Part IX, Forestry.

4. Government of India, Ministry of Agriculture, New Delhi, *Summary Report of the Study Team on Co-operative Structure in Tribal Development Agency Projects,* K.S., Bawa, 1973.

5. Government of India, Ministry of Agriculture, New Delhi, *Summary Report of the Study Group on Relief of Indebtedness, Land Alienation and Restoration in Tribal Development Agency Projects,* P.S. Appu, 1971.

6. Government of India, *Report of the Study Team on Social Welfare and Welfare of Backward Classes,* 1959.

7. Government of India, *Report of the Scheduled Area and Scheduled Tribes (Dhebar) Commission,* 1960-61.

8. Government of India, *Report of the Task Force of the Planning Commission,* 1973.

9. Government of India, *Report on Progress of Tribal Development* (1978-79), The Commissioner for SC and ST, New Delhi, 1978.

10. Government of India, *Report of the Study Team on All India Tribal Development Programme,* Planning Commission, New Delhi, 1989.

11. Government of India, *Report of the Study Team on All India Tribal Development Programme,* Planning Commission, New Delhi, 1969.

12. Government of India, *Report of the Committee on Special Multi-Purpose Tribal Blocks,* Publications Division, Ministry of Home Affairs, New Delhi, 1960.

13. Government of India, The Study Team on Industries and Allied Sectors in Tribal Areas (1978-83), Working Group on Tribal Development, New Delhi, 1978.

14. Government of Karnataka, Department of Tribal Welfare, *Tribal Sub-Plan,* Annual Plan 1993-94 and 1999-2000.

15. Karnataka State LAMPS Federation, *Proceedings of the Meeting Regarding Empowerment of Tribals. Held on 3 August, 1999,* LAMPS Federation, Mysore.

16. Karnataka Forest Department, *"Proceedings of the Meeting Held on 10, April, 1995 to Review the Working of LAMPS",* Office of the Principal Chief Conservator of Forests, KFD, Bangalore, 1995.

17. Registrar of Co-operative Societies, Bangalore, Patil Thippanna Committee, "Revival of LAMPS: A Report", 1993.

18. Registrar of Co-operative Societies, Orissa, Bhubaneswar, *Manual for LAMPS in Orissa,* 1981.

19. NABARD, *Statistical Statements Relating to the Co-operative Movement in India,* 1994-95, and 1997-98 Part-I, Credit Societies.

20. TRIFED, New Delhi, Hand Book: *"A Concept in Marketing Tribal Produce'.*